MW01002753

ALL THINGS ASIDE

ALL THINGS ASIDE

(absolutely correct opinions)

ILIZA SHLESINGER

FOREWORD BY MARGARET CHO

ABRAMS IMAGE, NEW YORK

Editor: Samantha Weiner
Designer: Danielle Youngsmith
Managing Editor: Glenn Ramirez
Production Manager: Rachael Marks

Library of Congress Control Number: 2022933706

ISBN: 978-1-4197-5940-6
eISBN: 978-1-64700-572-6

Copyright © 2022 Iliza Shlesinger

Jacket © 2022 Abrams

Published in 2022 by Abrams Image, an imprint of ABRAMS. All rights reserved.
No portion of this book may be reproduced, stored in a retrieval system, or transmitted
in any form or by any means, mechanical, electronic, photocopying, recording,
or otherwise, without written permission from the publisher.

Printed and bound in the United States
10 9 8 7 6 5 4 3 2 1

Abrams books are available at special discounts when purchased in quantity for premiums
and promotions as well as fundraising or educational use. Special editions can also be created
to specification. For details, contact specialsales@abramsbooks.com or the address below.

Abrams Image® is a registered trademark of Harry N. Abrams, Inc.

ABRAMS The Art of Books
195 Broadway, New York, NY 10007
abramsbooks.com

CONTENTS

FOREWORD by Margaret Cho

As you hold this book, know that you are in the mind of an exceptional author. Iliza lives her life critically and without illusions, and that clarity is hard-won from experience. I wish I was younger and had Iliza to guide me, but I still learn from her, even as someone who's older than her. I've learned that you don't have to quit when you are in pain, that you can write your way out of the suffering. That here is beautiful truth to be unearthed from the depths of despair. That the stupid can be smart, and that we put ourselves through hell for nothing. In her work, Iliza often casts herself as an Everywoman—and I understand that inclination—but the truth is, we would all be lucky if we were more like her. Every woman has something to gain from the Everywoman that Iliza presents in her hilarious and astute worldview.

Oh, I wish I had thought of that! is the thing that I think a lot when watching Iliza onstage. That is pretty much the highest compliment I can give. Or any comic can give. "You cope better than me." That is what that statement is saying. That is jokes. Coping. Complaining. Competing—with one another, but mostly, really, with ourselves, or the notion of ourselves. We have it sort of figured out, but even if we don't, it is entertaining nonetheless. And that is all that really matters.

INTRO

Here's why I wrote this book this way and why I wrote this book now.

Onstage, I love a verbal parenthetical. I love a "btw," and I love clarifying the previous with hyperspecific details and references and staying in the pocket on a joke. I love revealing that I, deep down, don't actually fully agree with what I just posited, but I didn't have enough room in that sentence to convey that, so here's the reality of it all. The problem is, in print, all the funny asides that color the story can be distracting. Too many commas and footnotes are annoying to read, right? Like, who *really* wants a clever footnote? That means you have to . . .

Read the sentence.

Keep your place on the page.

Then scan to the bottom.*

Then retrace where you were on the page and mentally get back into what you were reading.

It's too much mood shifting for a silly aside that wasn't so important that it needed to be included in the body of the text but was important enough to be included on the page and ruin your reading flow.

---

* Read the tiny addendum, that, tonally, takes you out of what you're reading.

I say, if the information was worth writing down, give it a proper place on the page. So I thought, *What if I just formatted my book differently?*

What if the structure of the book is built around how my brain really works? The bones that support the essay are there, but the meat, the tasty meat of it, the comedy and purpose and reflection, are in the indented asides;

> the deeply personal anecdotes, the confessions, and the context that give my point of view its color are all right there for you to see.

Plainly put, I wrote the type of essays that *I* would want to read. I give my—at times sentimental, but always honest and hopefully funny—perspective on everything, macro to micro, all-encompassing topics like aging, miscarriages, social decency, nostalgia, having it all, and, finally, I confront the most important question of all, one that I wish more people would ask themselves: *Am I actually an annoying person?*

But I'll be honest, this book didn't pour out of me. A few chapters were easy, but I wrote those, and then I found myself avoiding writing this book for months on end. It wasn't writer's block, it was self-imposed fear. I started to feel like I had nothing to say on the page. Like the weight of my views and opinions wasn't heavy enough to push against the weight of pain the world was in, that the gravity of what I had to say would be rejected because I wasn't, in a funny book, acknowledging the oppression, repression, and horrific situations people everywhere were and are dealing with.

The fear of being canceled by the Internet, the saccharine and often performative wokeness of pop culture are a constant threat to comedy. The endless sophistry of telling someone they can't have an opinion because they didn't consider everyone else's opinion wrecks progress and levity.

"I can't stand when they automatically put a plastic straw in my water."

"Don't drink any water; we're in a drought!"

"Oh, so you don't want Black Lives Matter protesters to have water?"

"Why are you posting about BLM when Israel is under attack?"

"Why are you even typing the word 'Israel'? Do you hate Palestinians? Are you Islamophobic?! Educate yourself."

"If you love being Muslim, why do you eat pork?"

"Why are you cutting out pork when it's red meat from cows that produce methane emissions? Do better."

"Oh, so you only care about cows but not trans lives?"

"So trans lives matter, but my right to have a gun in my home doesn't matter? SMH. Do your own research."

"Not everyone can afford a home; stop glamorizing unattainable wealth!"

"Why are you anti-glamour? Makeup matters! Be better!"

"WHAT ABOUT THE LIVES OF THE BUGS THEY CRUSH UP TO MAKE THE MAKEUP?! SAVE THE BEETLES, EAT THE RICH! Educate yourself and be better and do your own research, and I'm still SMH but also laugh crying and triggered!!"

But that anger, that fear of being misunderstood and ruined over it, is very real. And I was afraid anything I said would deliberately be taken out of context and used by someone who had no real agenda other than just making noise to cancel me.

I became scared and overwhelmed by all these external factors. I delivered the first draft of this book in September of 2021. So that would be the fall after about a year and a half of the world, specifically the US, being an absolute fucking *Gong Show*. Just a huge mess. Everything was so heavy all the time. Every Internet check became endless doom-scrolling through bad news tempered by only slightly less bad news. Reality was bleak, online rage and righteous indignation were rampant, people were on higher horses (Clydesdales?) than ever and angrier and more scared than I'd seen in my lifetime. Personal agendas took the place of civil discourse, conversations, and even scientific facts. Whatever you were politically or socially was wrong depending on who decided to observe you that day.

However you felt was discounted because whoever you were, you were blind to someone else's misfortune and, therefore, a bad person. Everyone was an expert on race, disease, the Middle East, and environmentalism, and almost everyone was right and wrong at the same time, all the time.

The paralysis many people felt due to the constant inundation of bad news was numbing. It *is* numbing. But, as an artist, I always try. It's my job to make comedy out of tragedy and to—get ready to clutch your pearls, folks—have a point of view and make people laugh.

Every time I sat down to write, I would get hungry or tired. At around twenty-one weeks pregnant, sure, a woman is always hungry and a little tired, but this wasn't about the baby. It was like I had mini depression but only when I opened this Word doc. This was about me giving in to the idea that anything you say either can and will be held against you or discounted simply because it isn't important enough. In 2021, the world was not a great place, and what I didn't want was for that to affect my writing and then you pick this up for a fun beach read in 2022, and it's all coronavirus/global warming/public outrage and other clickbait that's actually about something serious.

I felt I had nothing to say *on a page*, specifically. Onstage at a live show, I have plenty to say, my act is a living, breathing, mutating thing. But a book is forever. There was this overwhelming, personally imposed imperative that when this book came out, I would still feel the things I felt when I wrote the book over a year ago.

And thus: I put it off.

I found myself thinking, *Who wants to hear me lampoon everyday things in a book?* And then I thought, *But if I don't do it, someone else will. And then I'll be stuck trying to find an outlet to complain about whoever stole my ideas to write a book where I'm complaining. I don't care about those people or their malformed opinons. This isn't even a real conversation! I'm creating my own prison! Better to have tried, because most people can't even do that.* And then I thought, *I should be writing down all the little honest side conversations I'm having with myself because this is insane yet relatable and that's the funny part!*

And here we are. This book is an open book, so to speak.

I'm gonna talk about so many things that I think are either wholly relatable or weird, quirky things that, sure, might only happen to me, but it's in their weirdness that you get a peek into my life. And isn't that why you pick up a book from a comedian? To read what makes them tick, to see life through their lens, to laugh at their pain, to share in their similarities?

All things aside, let's have some fun.

NOSTALGIA

I coined the term "Elder Millennial" in my eponymously titled fourth Netflix special. Elder Millennials are now in their late thirties, could even be early forties. And those few years, from which I'm reporting to you live, are a real sweet spot. We are *just* old enough that our parents/society aren't talking as much shit on our generation as they did in previous years. However, we are *jussst* young enough that it's not weird if we do TikTok or, like, wear a crop top (right? It's still okay? Right? Maybe?). One of the cool things about getting older is that corporations are talking to us via our nostalgia and it honestly feels great! I love being catered to. The 2022 Super Bowl halftime show with Eminem, Dr. Dre, Snoop Dogg, Mary J. Blige, and 50 Cent was purely for Millennials. There was even a Quest ad featuring a fuzzy animal à la Chuck E. Cheese (or, for those of you in the know, Show-Biz Pizza) that actually made me tear up. UberEats used *Wayne's World* in their 2021 Super Bowl commercial. In 2017, Burger King used "Return of the Mack" to sell us deep-fried (*holds in American vomit*) mac 'n' cheese covered in Cheetos. The second that ad came on, I was right back at a middle school social, dancing in a circle with the five other girls in our chunky-soled MIAs. Tap into my nostalgia and I will hand you my money from deep in a memory-lane trance.

A new, weird way to gauge that you're aging is the amount of memes about your youth. My generation, Millennials, were the last generation to remember a world without the Internet. This is a point of pride that people have been talking about for a decade. We act as if we used to get all of our information from a coal-powered printing press before AOL came long. Because nostalgia used to be something that you came by randomly: "Whoa, a Zagnut? I didn't know they still made these. Gross." If you wanted to see an old episode, you had to wait for a rerun. Now everything is available in subscription-box form, on You-Tube, or in a streaming library. Everything you want to remember is a click away. Every logo, catchphrase, and piece of media you've ever loved can be reordered, reprinted, and recopied or is being revived by a network desperate for content. *Everything* is accessible because the Internet holds on to everything 4EVA. Fo-evah-evah. *Fo evah evah?* Now everyone gets to relive their youth whenever they want. You can relive it, revel in it, and rele-gate yourself to it for the rest of your life if you want.

My generation is obsessed with their own nostalgia. Like a narcis-sist obsessed with their own Instagram Story, that's how we feel about drooling over clickbait lists of products, music, moments, and clothes we used to love.

We go to *Saved by the Bell* pop-ups and still turn up Cascada's "Everytime We Touch" and think of Tupac as easy listening. We are the first generation to experience their own nostalgia via the Internet as curated by our peers. Gen X can, of course, go to an eighties night at a bar, but it's going to be promoted by some-one my age or younger who thinks the eighties was all neon *and no one from Gen X is going to attend because Gen X is now almost sixty! (Relax, I'm talking about elder Gen Xers.)*

This need for the warmth of "simpler times" as seen through the lens of your own youth was heightened in the pandemic and in the face of the global turmoil ensuing during and after (is this after?). Life has become so unnerving we wish we could go back to something comforting, to when life was simpler, when your parents could make everything okay again. Before you had to deal with your own insurance. Before owning a phone was dangerous. Before you realized your parents were right about almost everything. Before your neck hurt all the time.

A never-ending hot, chunky dump of a news cycle of feelings being facts, absolutism in identity politics, global pandemic, fires, droughts, hurricanes, Israel/Palestine, cancel culture, and unending civil unrest, all taking a backseat to the ever-present fact that the world is getting warmer and the rich are getting richer than ever before and there is less and less you can do about it because you are just going to be placed on hold before your call gets dropped. All with the added weight of knowing our generation is up at bat in terms of being adults, that we're the ones in our prime now . . . I can see why some of us chose to retreat to the online pacifier of a walk down memory lane. We need a break!

I follow nostalgic Instagram accounts with names like Nineties Throwback or I HEART the 2000s to see glimpses of products or memories I forgot I had. It's comforting. The past, when remembered fondly, is a safe place to revisit. But for that pure rush of nostalgia, it has to sync up with your memory perfectly. It isn't enough to say, "Remember malls?" You'd have to say, "Remember Things Remembered? Next to K·B Toys? In the nice mall with the ice-skating rink?"

"Remember being in middle school and wasting your allowance on collector's edition POGs and slammers?" This urge to demarcate one's generation from another's stems from the same desire people have to etch their heart initials into a post or tag a wall: It's a way of saying, "We were here. We were young. We did things we thought were new. We were here together. We felt happiness together." Maybe by constantly bringing up our nostalgia, by keeping it alive, we feel we can't be erased. We feel safe. We feel we mattered.

The Internet is replete with lists of nostalgic things, but I wanted to make my own.

The Things Almost Everyone in My Generation Remembers:
- Seeing Baz Luhrmann's *Romeo + Juliet* and wanting to be Claire Danes (even more than in *My So-Called Life*).
- The smell of Gap Dream, OM (wasn't it kind of spicy?), and my favorite, Grass.
- The smell of Bath & Body Works, specifically Country Apple, Sweet Pea, and Plumeria.
- Decorating your One Stars with Wite-Out, maybe even also painting it on your nails. It never looked that nice.
- Wanting a big Jessica McClintock GOWN but having nowhere to wear it.
- Big Johnson brand apparel. It was a cartoon about a skinny white guy who secretly had a huge penis so women with giant boobs were always around him. As children, we wore these T-shirts.
- College Bar hats from The Game. Remember these hats? It was just a hat with the embossed name or mascot of a big college. But everyone had one; the more worn in and disgusting, the better, and it didn't matter if you had no affiliation with that school. I had a UNC one simply because it was light blue. And

you got extra points if you got the University of South Carolina cocks hat, because then you were a fifteen-year-old with the word cocks on your head and it was very salacious!

- Listening to Eagle Eye Cherry's "Save Tonight" but not, like, fully relating to it.
- How expensive Abercrombie & Fitch was for a distressed shirt for a fake team from a fake athletic department.
- Wrist sweatbands as accessories.
- Spencer's/Gadzooks, where you could buy black-light posters and ironic T-shirts. You would also, as a thirteen-year-old, buy a lot of drug paraphernalia without having knowledge of the drugs. Lots of magic-mushroom tie-dye references, lots of incense. Lots of marijuana-leaf-themed pillows and hologram necklaces.
- *The Far Side* by Gary Larson and how smart and beyond your years you felt when you got one of the jokes.
- The best discontinued Gatorade flavor, Lemon Ice.
- The comfort of knowing your TV lineup for Friday night (TGIF) and Saturday night (SNICK).
- Wearing your YMCA softball uniform all day even though your game was at nine A.M.
- Wanting to re-create Alanis Morissette's "Ironic" music video in your car so badly, but having neither a car nor a camera.
- Slow dancing to Boyz II Men's "I'll Make Love to You" then breaking out into "Tootsie Roll," sung by a group called 69 Boyz . . . at a middle school social.
- Your mom relenting and finally buying a box of Pillsbury Toaster Strudels and you using up all the icing packets on one monster gooey Pillsbury Toaster Strudel and then having to grit your way through the remaining icingless pastries.
- Fruitopia (Coca-Cola's answer to "What is juice?").

- Orbitz, which was always weird and never loved. What *were* those little balls made of? Were they each a tiny universe suspended in space like that charm on the collar of that cat at the end of the first *Men in Black*?!
- Shopping at Brass Plum in Nordstrom. More specifically, that day you realize you are too old to be shopping at Brass Plum in Nordstrom.
- Ordering Airhead balls from that one entrepreneurial girl in your fifth-grade class. Her parents would take her to Sam's Club/Costco, buy her Airheads in bulk, then she would "customize" a giant wad of Airheads to your flavor specificity. You would eat half and get a little sick and try to save some for later, but it always got hair on it. Also Fun Dip—you always ran out of powder before you ran out of that chalky vanilla stick.
- And this one gets me . . . the voice-over of my dad behind the video camera, recording me and my brother when we were little. He would never make an appearance in front of the camera, only as narrator off camera. He was always in charge of slating, letting the audience know what was happening. Maybe for you it was a Hanukkah night or Christmas morning or just any day something special was happening. And even though it was a random moment captured out of an entire lifetime, it became archived family footage that was priceless. I can still hear my dad's voice saying, "It's February 22, 1987 . . . and we're all at Iliza's fourth birthday party at McDonald's."
- Also. Having a birthday party at McDonald's.

You can't have nostalgia without getting older. One inevitable part of getting older is watching a younger generation wear almost exactly what you wore without full acknowledgment that your generation did it first. But what is Gen Z supposed to do? Send a notarized letter to all Millennials acknowledging that everything in the Urban Outfitters 2022 No Fear collab summer collection was worn by Millennials first? Who cares? Because all generations take up old trends and rebrand them at some point. The nineties were all about sixties/seventies throwbacks—remember all the misappropriated HAVE A NICE DAY posters at Spencer's, all the platform shoes? Lava lamps? Bell-bottoms?!

But we're all guilty of it. This co-opting of fashion is its own rite of passage. We've all consumed versions of a previous generation's clothing with zero thought given to who wore it first. Because it doesn't matter, because guess what? When you're young, nothing anyone older says matters.

I have to go on record as having said this though . . . one thing I know for sure that my generation (give or take five or ten years older) did create is wearing clothes ironically. The idea to wear mom jeans and dad shoes—to sartorially inhabit something you, in theory, reject, therefore making it something you accept, was done by us first. I feel compelled to chronicle this achievement because I believe this is a major contribution to pop culture.

Starting around 1995 was the first time young people looked at clothing like a joke, used it to appropriate adult skin as a costume. I remember in the movie *Ghost World* when the girls are at a yard sale and Scarlett Johansson picks up a grandma hat Thora Birch is selling and says, "This was during your little-old-lady phase." We wore things ironically. It's ironic to be wearing an auto worker's button-down with the name FRANK embroidered on it. Why? Because your name isn't Frank and you're not a mechanic! It's cool to wear a vintage 1981 Washington Elementary 5K Run promo shirt because community events are dorky to a teenager and how could you run in that 5K? You weren't even born yet! Hilarious! It's ironic to wear short eighties shorts to a fun run because men/your dad seriously wore short shorts when they were young and the shorts are silly-looking and we think exposing men's upper thighs is weird (because of our society's deeply embedded homophobia and simultaneous repulsion at the idea of anything feminine on a man). The idea is it's something you shouldn't have or something that should be cast aside, but we are wearing it as a joke, which, therefore, makes it cool. In a way, people donning the clothing of an era they weren't around for demonstrates a lightly felt nostalgia for that time. These are the building blocks to the "hipster culture" that went on to dominate the early 2000s. Clothing that was so ugly it was actually cool. Tattoos that were so dumb they were funny. Yes, you all remember that one girl in your group, probably named Aubrey, who had a French moustache tattoo on her finger . . . well, she's forty now, with facial hair tattooed on her finger. Who's laughing now! Clothing that was so weirdly shaped, so asexual, that it almost elevated the wearer's intention. It wasn't always about sex and showing off your body—no, sometimes you just really wanted to wear these very thick, super high-waisted potato-skin-colored denim pants with a tucked-in asymmetrical blouse and an owl necklace! And all of a sudden an ugly girl named Mildred wearing that in Brooklyn was cool because she had a forearm tattoo of the little prince and worked at a nut-free bakery. No generation has ever wanted to be like their parents (until they finally bought a house, paid taxes, had kids, and then understood what their parents were talking about), but we were the first to appropriate adult culture *ironically*. Because being uncool is cool!

The endless generation wars are futile. Gen Z shits on Millennials. Millennials and Gen Z shit on Boomers. In the end, it's all clickbait.

It's all just content for you to click on that translates to a dollar for someone who has no real vested interest in the outcome of that debate. Every generation comes off as ignorant to the old folks when its members are still young, and no *one* generation, in its totality, is to blame for anything and everything. You could argue the seeds of global warming were planted during the Industrial Revolution. You could argue the seeds of social justice reform started when the first slave ran away or the first woman rolled her eyes at her idiot husband after he legally beat her. By attacking an entire group—younger or older—what are you really expecting? A mass apology? That the whole generation feels collectively terrible about their existence?

I personally think there is a gentility to the older generations, the Baby Boomers and whatever is left of the Silent Generation, that our modern world doesn't hold sacred. You aren't allowed to reflect on the past with rose-tinted glasses without first making it clear you comprehend how horrible things were for most people.

I think about my sense of patriotism and where it came from. I don't have a military family; I don't have friends or classmates who enlisted. Where, oh, where did I get a sense of such reverence for my nation? It came from my mother, who grew up in the fifties and sixties with a father who actively fought in WWII. She writes almost exclusively in cursive (which isn't taught anymore), loves and still remembers Gordon Lightfoot songs, instinctively stands and puts her hand on her heart when the national anthem plays, and she remembers historical dates and times, not just for the history of our country but European history. She told me they didn't have color TV until she was fourteen, just a blue, orange, and green piece of plastic to put over the screen to give the illusion of color. "It didn't fool anyone," she said. There is something sad about knowing the world she grew up in is gone. It's not about glorifying situations that were good for some, bad for others. It's about me wondering if my mom and dad are ever scared in this weird world that even the current generation is confused by. That's all. And maybe it makes me sad because I know I'll be in their position one day. I'll look around my meat farm on Mars from the oxygen pod that keeps my head separate from my body and I'll think, *This isn't my home . . . where'd all the animals go?*

Maybe it's because I haven't been in school for over twenty years or because I don't have a kid old enough to be studying, but sometimes it feels like no one is learning anything, no one cares how the world got to be the way it is, and history and context don't matter, all that matters is tech. All that matters is your profile or that you sold an NFT of a cartoon zebra smoking a blunt. Maybe it's because my mother is in her seventies, so she's connected to a time that is so far removed from what we know now, it feels like I'm passing up a free ticket to a museum when I don't ask her questions about her life and history.

I will miss having that connection to the past when she and the rest of her generation are gone. I'll miss hearing what camp songs sounded like for her. I'll miss her walking me through old photo albums of her parents. I'll miss being able to ask her what the sixties were really like, what the seventies felt like, what she remembers from the eighties. I'll miss hearing her say random Yiddish words her grandparents used to say because I'm sure I've retained only a fraction of them.

In 2021, I was on tour in Europe, getting off a train in southern Germany. I spotted an older woman, maybe in her eighties. She was dressed for another time, a total anachronism on this commuter train. She wore a scarlet cloche with a hat pin, perfectly curled short hair, and a delicate gold brooch on her long wool coat. She was dressed like your wealthy European grandmother. She looked at my mask and, in German, asked me something. I apologized and said I didn't understand. She switched to a native British accent and said, "I love your mask, is it Liberty?" I had no idea what she meant. I simply said, "No, a friend made it." (A fan had actually made it, but how would I even explain that?) She persisted, "But the pattern, it looks to be Liberty." Liberty is a famous designer store in London; they're known for their floral textile patterns. *What a thing to know*, I thought. I confessed I had no idea but hoped so, because it made me feel sophisticated. She disembarked, and I asked if I could help her with luggage. She said to me, "A Japanese man once told me the secret to a healthful life is to carry one's own luggage." Weirdly, I kind of already thought that, but having that woman reaffirm it made it feel as if that wisdom came from another time and found its way to me. (I arrived in London at the end of the tour and made it a point to take that mask to Liberty to ask them if it came from there; I had to know. It was not Liberty.)

Nobody who didn't ask *really* wants to hear about how it was when you were young except the people who experienced your youth with you. Those are the people with whom you can sit around every year telling the same story back and forth ad nauseam. Most people's eyes glaze over when you tell them how your day was; they're gonna go full comatose hearing a recap of where your first apartment was in Los Angeles fifteen years ago. Spoiler alert, it's gone and now it's just a windowless CVS.

I have a business idea. Sharks! I have an idea.

Listening to people tell personal stories you have no use for should be a sleep app. Gentle, monotonous information from loose acquaintances. Topics like:

VACATION
"I was in Santa Barbara with my cousin and his new girlfriend. We went wine tasting. It was so cute. They had, like, tables set up and, like, snacks, and you could look at the vineyard and walk around. We met this other nice couple . . ."

OTHER PEOPLE'S BABIES
"Maggie usually gets up at 7 but today it was 7:30 and she finished all her carrots, normally she'll only eat half of them but today she wasn't feeling well . . ."

OLD APARTMENTS
"I used to live right there! Oh, wow, they have a Jamba Juice. It used to be a Payless."

PERSONAL SCHEDULES
"I'm out of town this weekend but back the third, then we are gone for like a week with the in-laws, but I'm totally free from the eleventh on. Let me know when you're free."

A DOG YOU'VE NEVER MET

"My dog does the cutest thing when he wants treats. He does his paws like this." (*Does a gesture not even remotely as cute when reenacted by a human.)

Other snore-worthy topics include:

Literally any movie I haven't seen or the plot of any TV show I'm not watching.

"It's a documentary about a guy riding his motorcycle across the desert . . ."

"We did our fantasy draft all Sunday and into part of Monday."

"Here's a messy document with a 'tool kit' for you to access and decipher."

Anything about a teacher they had in high school.

Any detail about their dream, especially if you were in it. Oh my God, I DO NOT CARE . . .

Any story about "crazy traffic."

Any story about wait time at a doctor's office (unless you got right in with, no wait—that fantasy I always want to hear about).

Any description of a vacation they had from a place you haven't been and don't really care about.

FOOD I ONCE ATE. "Oh my God, this place in Denver has, like, the best tacos."

A RANDOM POLITICAL OPINION. Especially, *especially* if we already agree.

These are all intros to stories that are guaranteed to lull you to sleep. We can call it "Oh, That's So Fun," since it's the phrase people use to let you know they are hearing your story and approving of it without asking for further detail.

A moment of nostalgia, if it finds you when you're alone or with others who won't quite understand, is to be consumed quietly, like a sip of whiskey from a flask.

> Can we put a moratorium on the *gifting* of flasks? Be honest, when have any people in the twenty-first century ever really needed a flask, let alone this many . . . let alone a micro-industry of personalize-able ones on Etsy. You can buy a drink. Almost anywhere. And if you can't, then, I don't know, can you just get drunk *before* and maybe CHILL THE FUCK OUT for, like, the one hour you're at the memorial service? The ubiquity of this gift suggests the majority of people are alcoholics. And if you are an actual alcoholic, I think discretion eventually goes out the window. It has become the de facto gift for young men and butch lesbians. If you're between the ages of twenty-one and forty-five and from a suburb, you probably have a drawer of never-used flasks gifted to you on such auspicious occasions as **JARED'S LAST WEEKEND OF FREEDOM ~CABO~ 2017**. The men (and butch lesbians) we love deserve better and, given that flasks are often made of stainless steel, one should last a lifetime. Being drunk in a nondrinking public space is a little tacky as is, and what doesn't class it up is a twenty-five-dollar leather-bound, faux-flannel-print flask with **TANNER'S SLUT JUICE** embossed on it.

Nostalgia is personal, like political opinions or being high. You can try to include others, but be prepared for them to not be on your specific wavelength. Nostalgia is a popper of a high. And it can't last; otherwise it wouldn't be the past, it would be the present. You can never *relive* a night, you can never go home again, and you can't take it with you. You can only feel the *essence* of the past. Our society holds the fleeting feeling of nostalgia so sacred that even someone attempting to "relive their glory days" is seen as a loser. You never hear that sentence in a praising context. "She's back to her original weight, she went blonde, she's dating a great guy, and she's reading a lot, just like she did in high school. So great how she's really reliving her glory days. Oh, and she's also dating a seventeen-year-old, but he's basically eighteen."

Part of what made those memories so special was both the confines and releases of youth. You know what you probably aren't dying to do now as an adult? Go to a water park, drive anywhere, put on clothes after nine P.M. Play a game of full-court basketball. Get drunk creatively. Lie to your parents. Give a blow job. Be anywhere loud.

And what about raves?

To me, the appeal of a rave never had anything to do with the drugs. To me, it was an escape from the monotony of high school recreation. I didn't drink in high school. Why? Honestly, I never felt like it. Beer tasted like farts, and vodka seemed gross, so I just didn't care. And you know who peer pressure doesn't apply to? Anyone not trying to be cool. I wanted so badly to connect with people out in the world, outside of my school, so I would look up postings for local raves on homemade Angelfire websites, and I would go.

I would drive to a CD store in a strip mall off I-35 where you had to pre-buy an *actual* paper ticket. And then we would load into the car and drive thirty minutes outside of Dallas to whatever it was—a warehouse, an abandoned school, a theater. And we would dance. Okay, I danced, while most people made out or sold drugs. But I loved the dancing. It was a great way to let loose and be around people I didn't have to see at school. Were they all on the grossest Ecstasy cut with Tang and, Mylanta? Probably. But everyone was happy. Everything was bright. Socializing with young people beyond the one hundred kids in my grade was fun and exciting. Everyone wanted to meet everyone. Everyone shared bracelets, and I got to fall in love with electronic music, a love affair to which I am still deeply committed.

A few years ago, I decided I wanted to go to a rave. I hadn't been to a proper sketchy warehouse rave since college and, at thirty-six, with a mortgage and a wedding to plan, I decided it was the perfect time to Uber to an armpit of downtown LA and take drugs with strangers. The first and best part of a rave? The clothes. We went to a costume/stripper clothing store on Hollywood Boulevard to procure something neon and tight. Something about being able to afford anything you want (from a store where all the clothes are see-through and flammable) makes it less of an adventure. Somehow using a credit card attached to your own LLC to buy a DayGlo unitard with a cutout stomach hole feels a little less rebellious.

Once at the rave, we entered the warehouse, and it was mostly empty. Clusters of people gathered around the perimeter of the dance floor, but no one was really *on* said dance floor. It's so socially pathetic to enter a vacuous 3,600-square-foot space with party laser lights flashing and see no one dancing. So we got drunk. The alcohol was in those *extra*-shitty plastic cups, the kind that are frosted plastic made of like 100 percent cancer chemicals that you used to drink bug juice out of at camp. The shot glasses were the mini spit cups that a grocery store uses to hand out juice samples. About an hour in, with the party in full swing, we decided to find drugs. To be honest? I don't even know that I wanted to do them that night; it was more about the thrill of the hunt! How does one even ask for drugs? How does one ask for drugs when one is the oldest one there? People think you're maybe a cop and then a random fan recognizes you and then things are weird for you! A girl was so drunk in the bathroom I had to zip her pants for her. That night I was hoping to be the girl getting zipped, rather than the one doing the zipping, but I had to help her. As I zipped her pants, I thought, *Dissecting drunk-girl culture like this is the reason I have most of my Netflix specials. This woman basically bought me a house.* We never found drugs. Well, we never *bought* drugs. I *found* a tab of *something* orange in a baggie on the floor, but I am not desperate or cool enough to take bargain-bin discarded floor drugs. But zipper girl took it.

We heard there was a party a few blocks away, and so we left the warehouse in search of it. We were chasing the after-party, which never, ever works. If there is a lull between the party and the after-party, that's when people realize how tired they are and how insane it is to follow a stranger to a second location. What we got was exhausted after walking parallel to a freeway on-ramp in East LA at three A.M., realizing we didn't even know the address. I think we each thought the other one knew where the party was. Then we got an Uber. Then we got the fuck home.

Nostalgia is like an indulgent fragrance. You catch a hint of it off a guitar riff in a Blink-182 song. The whiff of Auntie Anne's pretzels can take you back to your hometown mall food court. Those first few bars of the Killers' "When You Were Young" can send you careening back to whatever dingy bar you and your friends frequented at twenty-three, when you were young. Then the car behind you honks and snaps you out of your daze, and you enter the parking garage at your orthopedist's because you think you pulled a muscle putting on your sports bra. You weren't even going to work out; you just wanted to get dressed for it in case you did.

I realize I just listed off a few pages of things from when I was younger. I wrote that to connect with anyone who may have experienced the same moments, but it's sort of selfish of me. Because the reality is? As I said, most people don't want to hear about when you were young. Sometimes I'll see posts from younger people of my same generation and it will be about something that I was just a few years too old for and I roll my eyes because it isn't my exact nostalgia and I don't care. Like, I've never seen *The Wild Thornberrys* because I was sixteen when that cartoon for children came out. So no, I don't care that the girl in it is also named Eliza! Stop telling me! I have also never seen *Blue's Clues* and don't care. Do you want to talk about *Are You Afraid of the Dark?* No, I didn't think so! I've never seen *Hannah Montana*; I will not "like" your post about it!

Even people older than you—people who lived through many of the same things you did but weren't *young* during them—don't care about your nostalgia. A Baby Boomer telling me about "The Day the Music Died" is as irrelevant to me as me telling a Gen Zer about the *real* day the music died, which for my generation was when Justin and Britney broke up.

You think other people will care because, for you, the memories are so vivid and interesting and part of your reality. And when it comes to sharing our stories—our wisdom!—with younger generations, you foolishly think, *Of course this girl will want to hear about my memories! Because I think I'm interesting!* After all, that TikTok sound bite she's jiggling to WAS OUR SONG! SWV's "Human Nature"?! That's not a fifteen-second dance! It's a whole song to which we choreographed a sixth-grade talent-show routine! This isn't ambient shopping music at Rite Aid! It's "I Believe" by Blessid Union of Souls! It's the song I had my first kiss to in Stephanie Chang's parents' garage! It's eternal! It's Toni Braxton blasting from the speakers of my best friend's '97 Cavalier, our bodies redolent of Pantene Pro-V and Body Shop White Musk Perfume Oil!

But then I think about how my eyes glaze over when someone older than me, unsolicited, gets that glassy look in their eyes and says, "When I was young . . ."

I was going to write that I'm a bad listener, but I don't think it's that black-and-white. I was bad at paying attention to math because it was hard. But I got As in English, because I liked it. So yeah, I think I tend to not listen to people because most people are boring, bad at telling stories, or just giving mouth-trash information. It's so rare to get new information; you have to seek it out. You have to filter out so much misinformation and so many half-truths to get to something real. Even when you find it, you then have to sift through all the boring parts—the preambles, the throat clearing, and the pointless personal anecdotes—to get to something that makes you actually perk up. Everything is designed to keep you passively engaged. Most news stories could be a sound byte, most articles could be a paragraph, and most limited series could be even more limited. But this book needed to be exactly as long as it is. I see the way people's pupils dilate when they get to describe a TV show they love. One of the worst social etiquette faux pas is asking if I've seen a show or a movie and I say NO, then continuing to go on about it, in depth. It's the verbal equivalent of watching someone masturbating, like, "Okay, this looks like it's fun for you, but what am I supposed to do since I can't join in?" (I was going to say it's like watching someone masturbate and your hands are tied, but that makes this way too sexually complicated.) There is a code phrase, by the way, for when that happens and it's "No, I haven't seen it, but it's on my list," which means, "No, I haven't watched it and I'm *probably* not going to, but I already know why it's great, so I don't need you to endorse it, I got it. Spare me. Please stop talking about it."

My friend came over with her daughter. Her daughter dresses, now, in 2022, at fifteen, EXACTLY as I dressed in 1996. It's uncanny. To add even more connections, she has the same coloring as me, the same long, curly dark-blonde hair I did, and there she was, standing in my living room in baggy jeans, a flannel, and one of those stretchy, loopy plastic chokers. *That's* when I knew, not so much that I was *old*, which is relative, but that I was aging, which is absolute. That I was, in fact, *getting* older, that it wasn't just an abstract concept as it has been for most of my life. You know you are older when you look at someone much younger and you say to them, "I wore that when I was your age." I couldn't believe the words were coming out of my mouth! My old mouth! For me, the discovery of that was so strong, the overwhelming reality that I'm not young anymore because there is a new, fully realized generation next in line . . . It was such a huge moment for me, such a massive realization as I stood at the feet (in the chunky-soled Steve Madden slip-on sandals) of the monolithic concept of time and my place in it. Yes, there's some part of me that had expected she would care. I thought, *I'm cool, and I'm a celebrity if you use the right Google key words. She is really going to care!* I thought she would say, *Really? What else did you wear? How did you act? What things did you do that I'm also doing because your generation was the only original one EVER?! ILIZA, YOU ARE SO COOL, AND BY ME AT FIFTEEN VALIDATING YOU NOW I AM HEALING ANY WOUNDS CREATED BY TERRIBLE GIRLS MY AGE WHEN YOU WERE MY AGE! YES, YOU CAN SIT WITH US!*

But she had nothing to say back. I couldn't blame her. Why would she? Much like when your parents' friends would gush, "You're all grown up! I used to watch you when you were just a little baby," and you're like . . . "Mkay, Gail, I don't remember that, but thanks for not letting me die in my sleep."

No, my friend's kid had nothing for me. She nodded her head, somewhere between meeting my eye line and her phone. "Cool." In the face of rejection, I don't often become unnerved; in fact, I become inspirited. I don't let things go simply because of a total lack of interest from a second party. If I did, then I wouldn't have gotten anywhere in show business. But on that day, I spared her the rest of my revelation and quietly dry-swallowed this landmark moment, knocking back my nostalgia pill with a grimace and dropping the subject.

But I wanted to grab her, *grab her*, and exclaim, "Lily!" (Her name is Lily, and she had better think it's COOL that she's in this book!) "Lily! Can't you see how huge this is?! Our experiences are connected, woven together through the fabric of time! Lily! We are mere specks in this cosmic conveyor loop of never-ending souls repeating each other over and over with slight variations! I'm in awe and saddened and honored to bear witness to the act of mere existence! Lily, can you hearrrrr meeee! Can you see how huge this is?! That I wore a cheap loopy plastic choker when I stood in your shoes, which for me were One Stars but for you are some sort of Nike collab?! Lily! Your fashion choices are not of your own discovery but rather the product of cyclical fashion and nostalgia rebranded and commodified for the next generation! We've been standing on the shoulders of pop culture forebears our whole lives! LILYYYYY!"

What would have been weird is if I said literally any of that. What also would have been weird was if I grabbed her and shook her. But I wanted to say all of that, and maybe give her a shove. But instead, what came out of my mouth was, "Yeah, it's just so crazy."

That was it.

So I'm gonna share another nostalgic memory that I hope you also remember.

I'm thirteen. It's Friday night, and my best friend is coming over because we are going to watch TGIF. We are going to make mixtapes by listening to the radio and recording songs directly onto a cassette tape. Then we are going to make up a dance and force—FORCE—my mother to watch us perform it. There are a lot of eight-counts and a lot of each of us waiting our turn while the other one has their "solo." We might play office. It's a lot of paper clip touching and writing memos on lined paper and using all of my mom's Post-it Notes. We also might work on our fashion line, then maybe we will rollerblade. I'll beg my mom to take us to Blockbuster. She will, but she won't pay the 90 percent markup on the movie snacks there because "we have snacks at home." (We don't—not like those.)

We are going to three-way dial another friend and the cute boy in our grade and ask him about girls he likes. We are going to call Time and Temperature just to have someone to call. We might make Rice Krispies Treats poorly. My mom bought me a box of Capri Sun pouches as a treat! We will puncture them wrong and spill them but still drink them all. Once in pajamas, we will list out our ambitions for the next day:

Make up another dance, of course.

Start a new business.

Make Pillsbury Cinnamon Rolls poorly.

One of us will fall asleep early after making a sisterly pact to stay up till midnight.

In the morning, we will not, it turns out, make up a new dance or start a business, and there were never cinnamon rolls in the house, so not sure why we thought that would happen. We will watch Saturday-morning cartoons on ABC, and her mom will come to pick her up. She'll come in and talk with my mom for a bit, which buys us *just* enough time to rehearse our dance from last night. Now we make both moms watch it and then beg them to let us sleep over again tonight. The moms will say no because one night a weekend is enough.

Nostalgia can be so ever-present in your mind that it helps shape your current thoughts. I think that your past reality and your current reality can exist, vividly, simultaneously. I think that's what feeling young is, and that's why we're so compelled to chase that feeling.

HAVING IT ALL

Here's a conspiracy theory for you: We constantly ask women about "having it all" to remind them that they don't, in fact, have it all and that they should spend more time focusing on what they don't have instead of what they do have.

But God forbid you have *a lot*, because then you have to endlessly verbalize how grateful you are so no one thinks you're a spoiled bitch. That's the truth. The need for successful women to make sure everyone sees them actively acknowledging how good they have it is built into our society's inherent disdain for women. It's not enough that she may thank the universe every day, send love notes to her friends, and donate to charity. No, if she isn't outwardly, publicly, loudly demonstrative of how humbled and grateful she is, then she is automatically a monster and then we can devour her!

The less secure women feel, the more they will focus on that insecurity, jockeying for ultimately unverifiable accolades, like which woman breastfed the best, who has the hottest beach bod or the shiniest horn, and toil over menial stuff like the less time they will spend on banding together, changing social climates, and being happy.

Moreover, it's weird that the goal is to "have it all," yet we are encouraged to try and downplay what we do have and to poke holes in someone else's seeming perfection. We love the idea that the perfect woman with the perfect marriage might secretly be an alcoholic lunatic. We love the idea that the beautiful woman grew up ugly or has some sort of inner battle she struggles with. We read celebrity interviews where we hope to find a shred of pain that we can cling to to reassure ourselves that "See? She's just like me, which is NOT SO GREAT!" God forbid you're an attractive woman who empowered herself by using every resource she had to carve out success. You then need to spend the rest of your life watering down your existence, explaining that you actually *do* have flaws and a hidden Achilles' heel like a suppressed stutter or one leg is just three cats stapled together, so other people feel better about themselves and don't hate you. It's disgusting. It keeps people forever striving, forever dissatisfied, forever insecure, and forever explaining themselves.

Think of how much less we would talk if we didn't feel the compulsion to equivocate our bold statements.

Oh, it's endless. Our society has become *so* sensitive that we now have to, often preemptively, cater to the incensed at all times rather than appeal to the sane people or just be confident enough in human intelligence to assume people don't assume the worst. "I love America" has to be tempered with "Not that our country doesn't have its flaws." We have been conditioned, particularly as women, to add the insurance of additional explanation to ensure that no one finds what we said offensive, even though it's *fully insane* (my use of "insane" was flagged in editing for sensitivity, lest someone who identifies as insane read this book and take umbrage) to take offense as often as people do. So we spend so much time making sure that we haven't offended people who had no business being offended in the first place. Pick a real hill to die on, folks, not every anthill you trip over. The endless tempering of ourselves we have to bake into every affirmative statement is exhausting and unproductive. We spend so much time letting people know we meant what we said but were fully aware of counteropinions even as we affirm our own stance:

"I can't stand wearing miniskirts." (Not that they don't look great on other women. I just think they are too short. But hey, girlfriend, if short is yo thaaaang, then you do you!) I would never judge anything! In fact, the rest of this book is just me apologizing for any previous statements where someone, somewhere may have taken offense! ALL SKIRTS ARE EQUAL, I AM JUST AN IDIOT, AND IF I HAVE OFFENDED YOU IN MY VIEW I AM SO SORRY, PLEASE LIKE ME AND DON'T CANCEL ME! I HAVE A FAMILY TO FEED! I CAN'T WEAR A MINISKIRT BECAUSE I HATE MYSELF! AND I HAVE MULE LEGS! There? Do you like me better now? I'm being so vulnerable, please, come toward me now that you know I'm half-mule and sniff my hand to see I mean you no harm!"

I also think the demand that we, mostly women, but this is for the general population as well, always have to be checking in to make sure we haven't upset anyone is another way we stay distracted. Pleasantries for the sake of manners in public are one thing; humans should constantly be reminding each other they can be civilized before humanity turns into one giant Best Buy

Black Friday zombie stampede. But I loathe the constant checking in. My life is bespeckled with endless texts of "ok," "heart," "cool," "thumbs up," "lol," "haha," "fire emoji." It's just us continually letting everyone know, "I saw your sentiment, I wasn't ignoring you. I am not mad at you." It's pedantic, and chips away at a person's energy. Small talk is exhausting.

I remember when I started taking Spanish in middle school and we learned basic conversation sentences. Just never-ending grilling from your teacher. *"¿Como estas?"*

And then you'd have to answer the only way you knew: *"Estoy bien."*

She didn't *actually* care how you were, and you were in middle school, so chances are you weren't self-aware enough to know if you were thriving or if life sucked. You would have to answer, from your limited vocabulary, that everything was fine. And then you had to HAD TO reciprocate: *"¿Y tu?"* And she would say what you just said: *"Bien. Gracias."* And you had to do this not just at the start of class, but even if you simply saw her in the hall. Just forever exchanging mediocre status updates with Señora McDougal. It only got slightly less mundane when we learned *"¿Y tu familia?"* and since I didn't know the words in Spanish for "My dad moved back from the East Coast and my brother lives with him now because he is having some trouble and my mom is seeing someone new, he seems great and it's nice to feel like a family and I didn't make Cheer Squad A and I think I'm gonna transfer schools because I might be drowning here," I would just have to tell her that they were also *"bien"* or *"bueno."* We never got too deep. I took seven years of Spanish and never really mastered tense shifts, so if you speak to me today just know that things are still in the present tense and things are still fine. And my family is fine. And I always confuse the word for "ice" (*hielo*) with the word for "sky" (*cielo*) and I can never remember, between *derecha* and *izquierda*, which is left and which is right; thank God pointing is universal. But if you need help ordering food, knowing the vocabulary words for air travel, or understanding the Spanish part of Sublime's "Caress Me Down," *soy tu profesora*.

Keeping women off-kilter is the best way to make sure they don't stay too focused on their own happiness.

Do you have the right serums? Is your partner that into you? Are you upsetting everyone around you? Are the books you're reading actually making you dumber? Did you choose the wrong Turmeric Wake-Up Latte powder? Is there a top out there that can complete your wardrobe and, thusly, you? Is your success holding you back from being other people's definition of successful? Is your sustainable cotton underwear subscription service secretly poisoning you?

If you didn't wonder about that before, I hope you're wondering about it now.

Also, you know what I'm tired of? Answering about my relationship status. When you're in your twenties and being interviewed, or chatted up by almost anyone, the endless treasure trove of inspiration for the interviewer, journalist, DJ, podcaster is "So, are you dating anyone? What do you look for in a guy?" The subtext being "Your current achievements and anything that got you to where you are in your career notwithstanding, what's going on with you having sex and finding someone with whom to keep having that sex? You know, your *true* purpose?" Then, once you're married, there's basically a five-year period where people still ask you, "How's married life?" Which is the most pointless, most banal, aimless question in the world. And WHO, in a casual conversation, is going to say anything other than "great"? But remember, ladies, you can't say it's too great, because then you're bragging about your married life, and, remember, marriage is supposed to be comically miserable—"Turns out I married a gorilla who can only read baseball scores!" It's lovely and your husband treats you like a princess? "Look at them bragging about their relationship. Her husband is too perfect . . . I bet he kills people. I can't wait till the police tally up that body count! That'll really take her down a peg!"

The other response I loathe is, after I give any answer, hearing back, "Only three years? So you're basically still a newlywed." "Now, you just recently, *sort of*, got married, right?" The idea here being no matter what your take is on your marriage, it's ill-informed, because the person across from you has been married longer, and, therefore, your answer about your life at this time is null and void because you don't really know what you're talking about . . . even though they just asked you how your marriage was. You know that I want to always say "It's great, and if it weren't, I wouldn't tell you because it's none of your business and you don't actually care! See me at the Civic Center this weekend! Tickets at Iliza.com."

I get that we all have molten-hot takes on relationships, but I'm done with questions about my love life. I can't help but feel the subtext is "You're a woman, so you are gonna have enough to say about this since marriage was and is, after all, the only thing that really matters in your lady life, that it should eat up some of our time. I mean, we can only talk about your art, process, projects, and perspectives on life, and business for so long, we have to have something to remind us you're just a dumb girl looking for love or annoyed at your husband! Come on, give us something juicy. You having any weird sex? Is your husband secretly an iguana? Confide in us here at the MissouriStarTelegraphTribune.Biz!"

Actually, the more I think about it, the more I realize every stage of the average woman's life is fraught with frustrating lines of questioning designed to do nothing but make you question your choices. "So, you got a boyfriend?" "When are you getting married?" "When are you having kids? I know you're in labor right now, but are you thinking about a second kid?" "Maybe men are intimidated because you're too successful?" "Well what were you wearing?" "You think *this* is hard? Wait until you have kids! Wait until you have *more* kids! Wait until menopause!" WHEN do we get a break from the endless projection? WHEN IS THE INTERVIEW OVER?! WHEN WE'RE DEAD?!

We don't ask men this question as much, if at all; we don't typically ask working fathers (aka just regular men who happen to be fathers) if they are trying to "have it all." By the way, you know who the original *wanters* of "having it all" were? MEN! Kings! Emperors! Conquerors! "God, gold, and gory," expanding a kingdom, overtaking people, building wealth, spreading a religion you sort of don't really believe in as a way of subjugating people. Having your legacy live on forever through sperm and random border placement! You want to know why most of the world is carved up the way it is? Why Brazil speaks Portuguese? Why we have a Church of England? Why Genghis Khan has over sixteen million descendants? Why most countries fight as they do? BECAUSE THE MEN IN CHARGE SPENT THE LAST FEW THOUSAND YEARS HAVING IT ALL AND NOT HAVING TO EXPLAIN IT IN AN INTERVIEW TO LIFESTYLELADYZ.NET! The pope wouldn't give King Henry VIII an annulment (which he wanted because his wife only had a useless girl, not a son like he wanted), so he CREATED HIS OWN BRANCH OF RELIGION SO HE COULD DIVORCE HER.

> And NO, women haven't all always been totally powerless, and YES, of course, there were powerful queens and empresses too. I feel like any time you bring up how oppressed women are and have been, someone is always quick to point out some uncelebrated benevolent warrior queen, as if you're igno- rant for not knowing twelfth-century Nordic history. "Clearly, you've never heard of Queen Bløød, who ruled for half a year over Flöörplån, which is now modern-day Oslo." This isn't a history book, and, for the most part, the guys came first (they always do).

You ask a woman, "Is it hard to have it all?" Women don't answer, "You mean commanding a spice trade, enslaving indigenous peo- ple, dominating the globe, and having as many children as possible with no regard for human life in general? Just trying to conquer outer space before Susan!"

No, it's much more personal. Having it all is impossible to quan- tify because, after all, what all is "it all"?

She has a husband, beauty, children, and a job she loves.

She has a partner, children, and a thriving dog facial business/deceased pet resin jewelry boutique.

She's divorced from that asshole, Bonathan, makes her own money as her own boss selling fish-scented pillar candles, and dabbles in Wicca.

She deliberately had no children, started a goose gym, volunteers at the library, and composes fairycore beats in her spare time.

She's rescuing dyslexic cats and reverse-catfishing Nigerian princes from a BlackBerry she's remodeling.

She is *power*-fucking dudes at night, microdosing mushrooms during the day. She's completely hairless and perennially wears winter white.

Her children are grown, and she's CEO and founder of an over-fifty shirtless all-female fight club. She hates her elbows even though everyone swears they don't notice them. They do.

She's running a thriving plant obedience training seminar, going on coffee dates with a man named Juul, and really into shell art.

She had a mild procedure done, and now her back hair gets tangled less when she dances in the moonlight. She's self-publishing her own interpretation of the alphabet.

She answers you with a coquettish laugh and says, "Well, I don't measure my life against the standards of others."

Which is a LIE. A weird lie we've all been forced into saying so we don't look competitive (which is somehow only a bad trait in women but lauded in male athletes and CEOs). We all measure what we have against what others have; that's how we know to want more!

Fucking duh.

You would never naturally come to the conclusion you need soft, hairless legs without seeing other women talk about how important it is. You would never decide you wanted to run your own business if you didn't see someone else thriving, running their own business. America raced to get a man on the moon because they saw Russia had already sent a man into orbit. No cavewoman woke up and thought, independently, *I need to get chestnut lowlights in the fall to soften my look*. You think every ball-player's wife did her own critical thinking and arrived at "I need a three-carat diamond ring" in a vacuum without seeing another wife having one? You think bodybuilders don't look at other body-builders as competition or inspiration? You think scientists don't look at other science . . . things and challenge *that* science in the name of science?! That's what an experiment is! You think body dysmorphia is something people had before we started painting and sculpting and touting "ideal" female body types?!

The key is to see everything, take in all the data, and, here's the hard part, don't let it drive you insane. Even if the person next to you is "perfect," so what? You're probably sitting next to someone right now who thinks you're perfect.

Or they feel bad for you. Or, even worse, they aren't even think-ing of you!

Having it all used to be very simple. From the first caveman to about the 1700s, for the average person, "having it all" was just not dying before thirty and having enough children to tend your farm. Maybe you had some land and crops and maybe a little bit of sheep meat for your birthday.

As humans moved from the nineteenth century into the twentieth century, "having it all" shifted to having a house in the city and maybe making money off a faraway farm you don't constantly tend to personally or making money in the city. Bicycles. Victorian-era photographs of your family posing with a dead relative, "taking to the waters" to cure rheumatism (or, probably, what was undiagnosed cancer), and having an electric lamp! Fast-forward to the fifties and sixties. "Having it all" became a house, a family, a vacuum, a color TV, a car, and a nice lawn and your husband's God-given right to mow it. Then you get to the seventies/eighties, where women entered the workforce en masse. Now "having it all" began to factor in careers for women. A career *and* a family and self-realization and shoulder pads and feathered hair and looking good while doing it.

Now, in the aughts,"having it all" cannot only be anything, but if you dare to define it, you will be canceled. How dare you suggest that for you "having it all" means a spouse, a house, kids, and a job when there are polygamous octopus trainers in tiny houses with adopted wolves and part-time gigs?? There is no one way to define "it all" because it's acceptable to express yourself in different ways now more than ever. And the way most people express who they are is with what they have, what they buy. Owning *things* is the easiest way to say, "This is who I am; this is what I stand for and a major component of my personality" without really having to actually say it. How else are people gonna know your passion if you don't get an avocado resin pin, a stuffed avocado plush toy, and avocado-printed pajama bottoms? PEOPLE NEED TO KNOW YOU LOVE AVOCADOS and that your love for them is a placeholder until you form real opinions on the news and society. "Avocado gal" is not a bio in real life. Unless you farm avocados, in which case . . . maybe get that trademarked because someone's gonna take it for an Instagram handle!

But what good is a life if you don't fill it with things that reflect how good that life is?

I think there are too many things. We have too many options for dumb things to purchase.

> Crocs, a shoe no one *needs*, come in over twenty colors, three of which are blue: Mineral Blue, Ice Blue, and Powder Blue . . . yet a cell phone charger, a thing everyone has, only comes in iPhone or Android; your only other option is to die, unincluded from a group text, without a phone.

And yet? These options only exist because we demand them. If people weren't buying Ice Blue Crocs, Crocs wouldn't make them. So I guess I'm mad at our endless obsession with having endless options.

> You know what we have too many of? Poke bowl restaurants. Not every shopping center block needs access to fresh tuna. Also, as my chef husband has pointed out to me, there is something weirdly off about fresh fish being offered in scoop form. "And how many scoops of tuna would you like?" Fresh water, fresh air, and fresh vegetables should be a basic human right available everywhere. Not fresh *overfished* ahi in scoop form in a strip mall next to a discount tire warehouse.
>
> Frozen yogurt. In 2005, Pinkberry opened, and people lost their minds over the idea that frozen yogurt could be tart. The last fifteen-plus years have been supercharged with frozen yogurt concepts. And yes, frozen yogurt is tasty, and I can

understand vegan or fat-free options, but . . . the toppings? Do they offer too many? Gummy bears? Why not just add full lollipops? You want ice-cold gummy bears on your yogurt? You want hard-to-chew gelatin that you end up just swallowing whole because it's ripping out your fillings? You need sour wilted unseasonal chopped berries all year round? Why not less and better? Why do humans need all options at all times no matter how limited in quality those options really are?

Dear Google, please make a button on Google Maps that allows me to search for local coffee that *isn't* Starbucks. I need a Starbucks filter. Why do we need a Starbucks one block from another Starbucks? Originally I thought it was to give the Starbucks employees at the first store a *different* store in which they could take their break. Then I learned it's because Starbucks would rather have a monopoly on the block than allow a smaller business to take even a small fraction. How depressing. We have too many Starbucks and too few options for local originality and independent commerce.

Also, do we have too many meal-kit options? Vegan, vegetarian, and "regular" is great, even though, if you really think about it, there's something so weird about personalized *mailed meat*. But it's as if these are less about food options and more about meal preparation options:

FRESHMAN: We send you all the ingredients you need to prepare a meal.

REFRESH: We send you pre-portioned-out ingredients so you don't have to think about cooking as you make your dinner while you half-pay-attention-watch *Carpool Karaoke* on your phone.

FRESHY FRESHY: We send you half-cooked beef and parboiled potatoes; all you have to do is finish them off when you're ready!

FRESHA: The food arrives pre-chewed and a little warm; all you have to do is chew the amount you want and someone will show up to massage your throat to help you swallow.

FRESHINA: The food is in a handy, BPA-free IV bag you can hook up to your vein whenever, wherever! This way your mouth can relax while your veins do the work!

FRESHONIA: It's an actual box of shit. Someone has eaten, digested, and crapped out your dinner for you.

FRESHAGRAM: This is just pictures of food other people are eating somewhere. It's Instagram.

But back to women . . . because even though your individual path to "having it all" is specific to you, the societal expectation on women has remained the same. Do everything, be everything to everyone, and look perfect doing it. It's unrealistic, and yet we all strive for it. We readily tell other women, "You don't need to do it all, fuck what everyone says and do you, sister chica mama boss rock-star kween!" But I don't know if we always heed our own advice.

The fact that no one feels like they "have it all" should tell us that "having it all" is a myth. You want to have it all and feel you have it all? You want to feel complete?! Sure, just step right over to this side, where the grass is greener, not like that ugly yellow grass you worked so hard to grow.

Look at Black women. Don't freak out. I'm white, and I'm saying the phrase "Black women," and I can feel your righteous fingers hovering over the cancel button. Just relax (other white women)!

For centuries, a European white aesthetic was put upon Black women. Right? Light skin was and is still to this day favored over darker skin in many cultures. Black hair was never allowed to be natural, it had to be "tamed," which meant ironing and harmful chemicals. All to make Black hair more like the hair of white Western women. Wide noses and bigger lips were mocked. Black bodies were sexualized and vilified and almost never celebrated. These are facts; this isn't some spin I'm putting on it.

In the 2020s, what is the aesthetic for white women we see in pop culture? The aesthetic is Black women. Bigger lips, bigger butts and thighs, combed baby hairs, etc.

> Anyone can have baby hairs; it's how you lay them flat them that counts. I have lots of them. If I had a cable drama, it would be called *Little Broken Hairs Everywhere*. It would be based on a harrowing book by Liane Moriarty.
>
> Baby hair, in the Black/Latina community, can be sculpted into swirls. If you're white, you can just comb it down and spray it, hoping it doesn't rebel and jut out like a bee stinger. But if you try to brush them down and you're white, it just looks like they shaved your head for brain surgery six weeks ago. I am constantly pulling on, patting down, battening down, and pawing at my baby hairs. I touch them a lot, and I also rub them.
>
> People scratch their heads (in cartoons) when they're thinking. I rub. I don't even rub my temples, I rub just above my forehead, right where horns would go. The hair is tiny and broken there. My husband calls it my "horn section."

I don't even think most young white women realize the look they are emulating/appropriating/stealing/mirroring, because it has been so inculcated into our culture at this point due to social media. And white people are raised to subconsciously (and sometimes consciously) think everything is *for* them.

I have to write here that while the Black Lives Matter movement and the subsequent long-overdue conversations about diversity, equity, and inclusion that it triggered nationwide was eye-opening for so many people, the part I could do without is the way being aware is wielded as a badge. There's now a constant out-woking competition when it comes to gender, cultural, politics, and race. It's inevitable that one might not know everything about another culture. Acting as if you've been informed from day one on topics like gender fluidity, trans visibility, Black history, Middle East relations, the global history of antisemitism, Indigenous people, Asian hatred, feminist struggles, etc. as a way of correcting past mistakes sort of negates the value of the education we should all be seeking. There is no way to possibly know everything. But what is possible is that we should all be open to hearing about someone else's plight without writing it off. The acknowledgment of ignorance and a willingness to try to correct it is the only way forward.

But the demand that darker women be lighter was and is racist. The demand that white women be tan is a trend. Regardless, the idea of changing your skin color to be acceptable or attractive de rigueur is wrong and unfair and insane. Let alone the fact that believing your skin tone makes you superior to someone else is a harmful idea derived purely from a baseless social construct. I do want to say that mocking a darker woman for her skin tone is deep-seated racism that carries with it hundreds of years of hate and oppression spread through hundreds of cultures and countries. Calling me "Casper" or "gross and pale" doesn't have the same sting to it, but trying to make anyone feel uncomfortable in their skin because a magazine is trying to sell you a trend—even making fun of redheads—is small-minded and unevolved.

I am saying this as a proud pale person, a person who turns almost purple in the winter. I have the privilege of not caring if you think my skin color is ugly, and I recognize that not everyone has that privilege. But either way, you're weird for caring about anyone's skin that much. A great fake tan does wonders, but it's not sustainable. Forever glooping on self-tanner (which, I don't care what advancements scientists make, always smells like dirty cookies), spending hundreds on spray tans . . .

> Why do I remember almost no one having a *realistic* fake tan in the mid-aughts? Everyone wanted to be tan like the *Jersey Shore* kids (fully grown adults), but no one wanted to concede that they were able to tan so deeply because they were Italian. I feel like every Myspace picture of twentysomethings partying was just yam-tinted white people. Rust-colored masses, with splotchy "sun-kissed" faces, acting like it was normal to look like you slept on a nuclear reactor. A whole generation of women with self-tanner caked into random skin folds and haphazardly painted-on ankle bones looked like the annals of an ant farm crammed into the wrinkles of their wrists and toe knuckles.

It's crazy to expect someone to be lighter when they're dark, to have flowy, long, straight hair when it's kinky or even curly and wispy! I have that kind of hair—one drop of moisture in the air and I look like Tom Petty growing out a perm.

If you live long enough to see trends come, go, and come back around, you might start to sour on the idea of pop culture. Because these trends always require three things:

MONEY: to buy into the hype

ENERGY: to care about the hype

TIME: to dedicate to spending the money and expending the energy on being part of the hype

> Time, also, as in you have the time to dedicate to the trend because you aren't thinking about more pressing things, and time as in it's on your side because you are young. No one cares about a trendy Elder Millennial. At forty, you're now in cool-mom territory even if you're not a mom.

No matter who you are, you are constantly being told to strive for the opposite. Are you rich? Give more money away. Are you poor? Get rich, quick! Do you have things? Downsize. Are you not treating yourself enough? Get that boat! Get this credit card! Rack up debt! Use Krabapoo, our debt consolidation app with a cute, weird name that belies the severity of giving a random app all of your banking and personal information! Create a budget for your spending problem! Got a bunch of stuff but feeling depressed about your life? Try these self-help books! And while you're at it, grab yourself a sugary coffee drink at one of five thousand area Starbucks locations! There are voices out there reminding you that you are never quite doing life right. And those voices are there by design. Because the more you doubt your path, what you have, and what you want, the easier it is to sell you more crap. "You would have it all if you just had this one blender . . . if you just let this one app startup tell you when to breathe and what to eat . . ."

I'm not a nihilist, and I'm not a pessimist. I'm a realist. And the reality is? Almost everyone is lying to you almost 100 percent of the time, and almost everything is a scam.

EVERYTHING IS A SCAM

Originality is rare. Innovations are important; everything else is just a cheap knockoff. That goes for products, people, ideas, and rhetoric.

Almost everything in life is a scam. You go through life unable to avoid these scams; the key is judiciously choosing which ones to buy into that will create the smallest headache.

You know what's a scam? The "stylus" pen. Every few years cell companies reintroduce this writing device that was around even pre–cell phone. Sometimes it comes alongside the phone; sometimes it's stored *in* the phone. Apple had the Apple Pencil. A few years ago, Verizon had a program where you could just come into a store and they'd fuse one to your hand, if you added a family line.

In the nineties, my mother had a personal organizer device called a Zaurus. It came out right before the Palm Pilot and it was a mini digital Day Runner with a keyboard and a screen. In it, you could keep your contacts and calendar, and if you fed it gasoline I think you could connect to the Internet. Looking back, I think it's pretty cool how tech-forward she was. Nowadays, despite her being a wizard at Excel for planning family

Thanksgivings, she sends me no fewer than five DMs a day accidentally in "vanishing mode" about dachshund puppies.

But I remember she would always call it her "Zaurus," never her "planner" or her "organizer," and she was always asking me to fetch it for her whenever she needed information. "I need Gail Goldstein's number," and then she would declare, like a wizard to an apprentice, "Iliza, the time is upon us!" *lightning crash* "HAND ME MY ZAURUS!"

What really changes is the price of the phone and the poking stick itself. What stays the same is that people keep being "wowed" by something that comes around every three years, they buy it, lose the fucking pen, and end up using their fingers.

I feel like the 3D and vampire obsessions are two things in entertainment that keep coming back around. Like every ten years, executives are like, "All right, new group of horny weirdos, let's revive this corpse." Until we *Black Mirror* 3D technology into our actual eyeballs, people will forever look stupid wearing glasses or headgear so they can enjoy the thrill of a half-see-through dinosaur "coming right at ya"!

Workout clothes are a scam.

You are the average person, right? You are probably doing, what? An hour of yoga a few times a week? Streaming a forty-minute dance cardio class off of your phone? You're doing ten minutes of running and crapping out halfway through that fifteenth sit-up? You allowed yourself to skip the cardio because you promised yourself a "really good stretch," but now you're sitting in a broken pigeon pose checking your phone. You do your class and then eat protein pancakes with a mimosa. The last mile you *truly* ran was in high school.

You don't need water-wicking Gortex shark wings stitched into your shirts. You don't need "movement technology" or however they want to spin their version of cotton interlock. You know what's super moveable and breathable? A T-shirt. Soccer shorts. That's what you need; that's what you deserve. That performance-focused, poly-blend, hyperabsorbent ninja-skin bra came off the assembly line ready for a premier athlete, not to be worn to WHOLE FOODS ON A SUNDAY!

Athleisure wear is athletic apparel you can sit in. It's also pajamas you can work out in. The idea of comfortable activewear is that *if* there's an emergency that requires you to bolt, sweat, or pulse for ten seconds, you are ready to rock. I blame their rise in popularity on viral videos of flash mobs. People needed to look normal but be ready to dance at a moment's notice!

> The original athleisure wear came from kids who played weekend sports. Do you remember? You'd finish your YMCA-regulated basketball game and then just wear that smelly uniform *all* day as you rode around town with your mother running errands. You had seen action that morning, and you were dressed and ready for more action! Dressed and ready to hand her her Zaurus!

Athleisure wear is our futuristic civic uniform, and everyone is wearing it. Honestly, people take a thirty-minute low-impact cardio class, and they look like they're dressed to walk on Mars. You walk around any suburban outdoor mall and see whole families waiting in line at Bubba Gump Shrimp Co. dressed like the Jetsons. HOWEVER. What *is* real is how comfortable the outfits are and the way a cute workout outfit makes you feel, and I guess that's half the battle when it comes to exercise motivation.

Moving on to even more casual clothes, you know what's a rip-off? Matching sweatpants/sweatshirt sets.

So cute, right? I get it, we all want to be streetwear chic flying first class in a matching sweatshirt/pant combo with an iced coffee. The idea is especially alluring when you look on Instagram and the clothing company reels you in by lining up all the colors they offer in a very satisfying gradient color scheme:

Deep Black, Light Black, Midnight, Mystery Plum, Terra-Cotta, Burnt Cinnamon, Charred Cinnamon, Regular Cinnamon, Fake Tan, Solar Peach, Mantequilla, Cream, Oatmeal, Vape Cloud White, White, Overly Woke, Cancel Culture Committee, and Talbot's Clearance Sale. And the top and matching bottom are sold separately. Pants are $138, and the matching sweatshirt is $208. For, basically, a public school PE uniform that has some random signature detail on the knee, like stitching that says TOKYO, NY, LA or PEACE sewn onto the shoulder or something meant to sound vaguely translated, like PANIC RUPTURE. So now you're in a full OATMEAL-colored KITTEN ARMY $346 sweat set, and you look like a federal inmate during yard time, but whatever.

WHY are sweatpants more than 100 dollars? Why are any sweatpants now the price of a cheap phone?! WhaT ArE YoU tALKing AbOuT?! When did EVERYTHING get so out of WHACK?

And you spill food on it. Now the top has to go to the dry cleaner, and it will forever be "faded oatmeal," and for that matter you could have just gotten a Vape Cloud White top. For that matter, you should have gotten a darker sweat set since a full outfit of light colors is basically spitting in the face of marinara sauce–colored fate! You will spill on your light outfit! NOTHING CAN BE MATCHY-MATCHY FOREVAAHH!

Most tank tops are a scam.

If you are an average person, clothes are not meant for you. If you have any part of you that deviates from model measurements, clothing is more of an idea than a practice.

The idea is that it's a thin-strapped tank top you can "throw on" casually.

> The practice is you double-sided-tape-sticking the life out of your bra, praying to God this tape is enough to force the tank and bra to stay together.

The idea is that it will just hang off your frame.

> The practice is you tugging at your bra straps before, pinning, gluing, *welding* the straps together in the back to form a racer-back bra, hoping they stay put under the one millimeter of fabric the tank provides that makes up "the back."

The idea is the fabric intuitively knowing what part of your breasts to cling to.

> The practice is you forever adjusting the tank so either the bra straps show or the tops of the cups of your bra peek out.

The idea is "any woman can wear our tanks because we have designed the perfect tank."

The practice is you conceding to the fact that you are not the hipless, breastless fifteen-year-old the company modeled the tank top after and you need to wear a bra and it's going to show.

The idea is the notion of inclusion has been woven into this strappy tank top.

The practice is you becoming okay with your bra showing.

The idea is that this tank doesn't show any part of your bra, and it's all so effortless.

The practice is you convincing yourself that it's empowering to let it show but really, deep down, you'd prefer it didn't because your bra is ugly and we've been too conditioned to not show underwear to start showing it now.

Because the majority of tank tops are designed without a woman's bra in mind (just like I've found many pumps and nursing bras are designed with a hunchback in mind), they simply don't account for the fact that they are cut so narrowly that most bra straps show and most women allow that to happen not as a deliberate fashion choice, but out of exhaustion.

What about those tanks that are cut so narrow in front they basically look like you're wearing a racer-back sports bra backward? In fact, many designers design as if bras aren't a factor because, to them, your body is wrong. You aren't a model, you aren't tall and thin and lanky, and you don't have the dimensions of a praying mantis. So while they encourage you to buy their tops, the way you wear it is up to you, aka your problem. Because even brands don't know how to deal with bras. Go online, find an impossibly cool tank top, and look closely. That model is wearing a bra, and the straps have been photoshopped out. No matter! I'm sure there's a solution out there:

"Go braless!" Cool . . . Braless is great if you don't plan on dancing, walking, being thirty-five, or moving at all.

"Go strapless!" Yes! You know how you really need bra straps to hold your boobs up? Well, just don't! Spend the entire evening negotiating with that strip of dried superglue masquerading as a built-in bra shelf that's supposed to support you.

"Use tape!" Of course! What woman doesn't want to mummify herself in thirty dollars' worth of tit tape, only to hold her breasts up an eighth of an inch?! Also? It's so fun to rip off your breast skin at the end of the night.

"Let it show!" Sure, you could let your zombie-gray-beige, pilled, old bra show if you want to look like an exhausted Midwestern carnival worker on a smoke break.

Most skin-care promises are a scam. They don't lie to you, though. They never say "will erase lines." Instead, they use vague language like "promotes the look and feel of younger-looking skin." What the hell does that actually mean? Promotes? Like it sends out an email blast? "The look of younger-looking skin" is subjective. Sixty is younger than eighty; do you want to look sixty? And feel? They can't possibly know how your own skin feels to you.

I think expensive eye makeup is a scam.

I know, makeup TikTokers everywhere are triggered. I have no problem with makeup.

I think hoarding makeup you use for a week then moving on to another variation of "sparkle tan" is absurd, stockpiling it as if it's a collector's item that goes up in value. It's a plastic case filled with a dollar's worth of powder, and you're paying sixty dollars and barely using it. And people do this because people, online, like to look at people's excess. Americans find it comforting to own a bunch of crap and to look at other people's crap if they can organize it well.

You ever see the people who obsess over collecting candles or matching bath products? No one can relax that much in a lifetime, yet thousands of people have shower bunkers filled with giant plastic tubes, bottles, and jars of body scrubs, soaps, washes, and lotions. People fill their hall closets with a monastery's worth of scented candles just to say they have captured all the smells of Christmas! So what's the rule? It's not hoarding if it's alphabetized? It's not excess if it smells like Vanilla Berry? Go on Instagram and look up #candleday or #showertok.

There is no color you can get at say, MAC, that you can't get at Walgreens. No one has ever thought, *Her brown eyeliner looks cheap; I can tell it's not YSL.* We're dewy, we're matte. We're contoured, we're blushing. We're sparkling, we're subtle. We're glittery, we're muted. We are forever at the whim of a company that names its products things like "Big Girls' Night Out" and "Golden Hangover."

Fact: The five-dollar Wet n Wild palette you bought ten years ago still gets the job done. You know what never goes out of style? A brown Almay eyeshadow palette.

Ever really think about the name Wet n Wild? It's geared toward people at a lower price point and the young. Meaning we want our women who are on a budget and our teenagers dripping wet and feeling wild/horny, now put on this blue eyeshadow, get out there, and give the best-worst hand job of your life, you juicy empowered slut!

Hair growth oils are a scam.

You know what everyone uses because they work? Sunscreen. Toothpaste. Soap. You know what you never really see promoted by major beauty companies? Hair growth serum. It's usually promoted by someone whose hair grows long naturally. If your hair is fine and breaks at the ends and doesn't grow long, it's probably never going to. You're just gonna make it oily.

> My hair always looks fine. It is fine, as in delicate, but I mean "fine" here as "perfectly acceptable." My hair always looks FINE unless I have extensions in. My wedding day, it was FINE. My mother starts literally every FaceTime with a commentary or excuse about her hair. AND HER HAIR ALWAYS LOOKS FINE. I think she passed this neurosis on to me. I touch my hair. A lot. Not even in a funny airhead-combing-through-it way. In an "I have six hairs and I'm positive they are all out of place and if they weren't they are now because I keep pawing at them" kind of way. No one is ever going to be blown away by the quality of my hair and no one is ever going to think it's bad enough to say anything. It's just there. The hair is just there and no one cares or stares, so there.

The idea of tea is a scam.

Wars have been fought over the farming and distribution of it. Imperialism, both British and Chinese, was spread while consuming it. Our own nation's revolution was sparked by dumping it in Boston Harbor. It can be herbal, ancient, medicinal, floral, or iced.

It can be pressed into a heart-shaped charm and shipped to you in a personalized bag or served in an expensive, hand-carved wooden box; it can be thousands of dollars and rare, or $3.95 and mixed with lemonade, served as a luxury item or sipped at a ceremony. But for most Americans, it's that thing in a packet that comes for free next to your instant coffee in a hotel room.

Tea has come to symbolize slowing down and taking a moment. It's meant to be sipped by a rainy window while you read a book and eat tiny cakes.

Tea in the morning represents a moment of decompression. It's what you drink to wind down; coffee is what you drink to rev up. Tea is a warm bath for your stomach. Coffee is what you chuck down your throat to get your gears moving and pump out a hot dump.

Tea is a mood calmer for those drinking it and a mood killer for someone watching you order it on a date. If you're ever on a date (with a girl or a weird dude) and they say, "I'll just have a hot tea"? Pack your genitals, because she's going to order a hot tea and tell you about her parents' divorce. For the most part? No woman has ever ordered a hot tea at the end of a date and then gone on to stay up all night and have great sex. No one orders tea unless they're sick or don't want to drink.

But I want to be a tea drinker because those who opt for tea just seem like they have it figured out. They seem centered, like they know something about health and overall wellness that I don't. Calm, detoxed, focused, anti-inflamed, sleepy, awake, imbued with Eastern wisdom, inspired—whatever you're feeling or want to feel, there's a tea for that. Do you want to sleep? Do you want to dream? Do you want to stay awake and daydream? Do you want to detox while sleeping? Do you want to be forever connected to the five strangers who were *also* booked on your Ayahuasca tea retreat that weekend? Do you want to say the word "rooibos"? There is a tea for every season, for every mood, and from almost every culture. I love the idea of coming off so wise and centered and in touch with my body that I drink a tea no one has ever heard of and I carry it with me to a restaurant. As if my health and wellness is so researched, I know exactly what combination of leaves to drink for my body.

> "What's in the velveteen satchel on her hip?" they whisper. "Oh, it's a precise combination of Da Hong Pao, Silver Needle Ant Nipple, and matcha with a gram of Celestial Seasonings Sugar Cookie Sleigh Ride. It promotes the feeling of younger-looking skin . . ." And then I laugh and sip! And savor!

I followed a yogi on Instagram for about a year. She had a thoughtful handle that let you know she was on a journey and yoga was her mode of transportation, something like "Lana's Path" or "Discovering Megan" or "Locating Janice" or "Where the Hell is Julie?" I liked her calming vibe; she made me feel like everything could be fixed with a deep breath and a morning yoga practice. Every morning she would do an hour of deep breathing and posing in her cozy living room and then post her practice online. She was so lithe and so toned; physically she carried no extra weight with her, and I just knew that applied to her mind and soul as well. I loved how effortlessly bohemian she looked in her leggings and homemade leg warmers.

> I just knew the leg warmers were handmade and gifted to her from another yogi, a hot dude named Kah, who lived just down the mountain (I wanted her to live on a mountain). From the pictures she posted, her home seemed so quiet and lived-in. I imagined she kept a fox as a pet. I imagined she only ate thoughtfully.

There's no way she'd ever gotten a lunch hangover or had a Cinnabon even though she wasn't hungry but it was in her terminal next to her gate and her flight was delayed. She probably never even had a delayed flight because she was able to view minor inconveniences in life as "part of the adventure" and not a regional airline FFFFFUCKING her really hard.

I wanted to have mornings like hers. Calm, intentional, healthy mornings.

Not puffy-faced, alarm-clock-fueled, GET-TO-THE-AIRPORT-BY-SIX-A.M. mornings on only two hours of sleep because I just had to stay up and rewatch the whole first season of *Schitt's Creek*. AGAIN.

She would post her long yoga sessions as sped-up videos, so you could watch the full hour in a few minutes. She even ate during her workouts. That's how slow and mindful they were, that she could pause to take intentional bites that would nourish her movements, being mindful of her breath. She wasn't gulping down grape Powerade midpant.

From what I could tell, she was eating oatmeal. Probably wasn't even just regular oatmeal like I eat. She was probably having something she mixed herself, a *forest-floor* day starter made with amaranth seeds, straw, flax, and some bark niblets. All raw. With a little bit of turmeric, you know, for a sweet treat.

She ate out of a thick terra-cotta-colored earthenware bowl. I wouldn't even call it "eating"; she was *nurturing* her cells, empowering her muscles via nourishment from a locally lathed bowl. You know she supported local small businesses, a pottery shed run by her friend/mentor and paramour, Io (pronounced "Heeeyaough"). She only ate wholesome things.

> She wasn't choking down a cold-in-the-middle breakfast sandwich, rage scrolling through a news feed.

So I set out to do what she did. I was so enchanted with her practice, and I knew, I just knew, that if I ate breakfast out of a thick bowl while doing yoga, it would be an instant path to enlightenment.

I set up my yoga mat, I pulled out some warm socks, and I made a bowl of oatmeal and a cup of tea. There had to be something to this; I mean, she did it every day! I took a bite—oops, I didn't make enough hot water; now the oatmeal was only partially cooked and a little thick, but whatever, oats is oats! No time to reheat! I had to get to the yoga! I had to begin my journey! I took a sip of hot tea. It was too hot! I burned my mouth and throat. That's okay! It's all part of the voyage; now I could gnaw on my peeling inner cheek skin as a side activity in plank pose.

We did our first series of intense stretches and then moved into downward dog. Down I went and up came that hot tea and, with it, my oatmeal. Oats in my throat! Stomach acid sizzling through!

I came back down, stretched some more. Heartburn in the morning, ugh.

> Yeah, I should definitely have put the oatmeal back in the microwave. Is it hot in here? Why am I wearing leg warmers? It's ninety-five degrees outside in Los Angeles; our muscles are always warm. If I pull a muscle, it's gonna be because that

muscle wants me to know it didn't want to be disturbed, not because it wasn't warmed up.

She was on to a vinyasa flow. My stomach felt raw, and the phone was ringing. My dog, Tian Fu, had also made her way onto my mat for a nap. Cardinal rule of owning a dog is if they lie down anywhere ever, you don't move them because they look so cute it's worth the disruption of your routine. Ugh, now I'm burping hot tea.

No one should be this hot five minutes into a yoga class. I crapped out. I took the warmers off my legs. I chugged a glass of water, and then I drank a huge cup of (iced) coffee: Time for a reset. I put on a Ying Yang Twins Spotify playlist and did a twenty-minute cardio blast workout, and then I unfollowed Yogi Janice. I don't even like tea. I don't have the patience to be someone else.

Big alarm companies are a scam.

Most alarm companies are a lie. One in particular, which I will call ICK (because that's how I'd rate their service) in place of their company acronym, has made it on my lifelong shit list and opened my eyes to what most of us actually get when we pay for "security."

We had their system installed as an extra precaution because I have a stalker. After weeks of alarms randomly going off and sensors dinging for no reason (and no, we didn't have a ghost), we asked ICK to cancel our service. They wouldn't allow that. They would, however, schedule endless maintenance visits "with a technician due to arrive between the hours of eight A.M. June 1 and 0-dark-thirty next Christmas." So thank God the horrible story I'm about to tell you happened.

You don't need to be famous to have a stalker. It happens to so many people, but probably mostly women who make the mistake of using the Internet or leaving their house. My stalker has stalked me for years. He has stalked me in two states, and he has found me in my last two homes. In fact, him finding me at my last house was my motivation to find a new house with a gate. It was late in the evening, deep into the pandemic, around ten thirty P.M., and Tian Fu started barking: Someone was at the door. Unnerving because, at the time, we basically lived at the top of a hill up a donkey trail even the post office didn't recognize as an actual street. It was great for privacy but horrible for practical accessibility; if I wanted my mail, I basically had to send a raven to a PO Box to retrieve it. Moreover, my house wasn't listed under my real name. So it wasn't something one would stumble upon. We pulled up the security camera, and it was him, my stalker. *How did this psycho find my house?* We immediately called the police and ICK. Why did we also call ICK? I don't know. I think that false sense of security is what you pay for when you use an alarm company. The idea that a middle-aged man in a dented Prius armed with a flashlight is going to lay his life on the line for you I guess affords some comfort. The police were dispatched, they were on their way, but where was ICK? They had a local outpost; it was the reason we'd bought a security package from them; they should have responded within minutes of a call. It's what we paid for, every month. We called them five times that night. Five! Each time painstakingly detailing, again, what was happening, that it wasn't a cat who'd knocked over a trash can, that it was a person stalking me against whom I had a temporary restraining order.

> I really wanted this guy to go to jail. It had been years of his bull-
> shit, and he only ever got more aggressive in his attempts at
> reaching me. This time, we would later find out, he had broken
> into a neighbor's garage, stolen a few items, and stalked me for

days before showing up and leaving those items as a gift on my doorstep. How do I know he stalked me and tracked me? Because part of his "schtick" is that he loved playing cards (is he a Batman villain?) and he would frequently, in his long, incoherent rambling posts on Facebook, where he tagged me and talked a *lot* about shooting people, also incorporate the theme of playing cards, posting pictures of cards, talking about cards, etc. Makes total sense, because you know what my stand-up specials and the nine of clubs have in common? NOTHING. Anyway, he was obsessed with playing cards; it was even noted in the police report. What's double creepy is that two days before this incident I took Tian Fu for her morning walk. We always took this private, secluded path that led to a dead end. Only people who lived in our neighborhood ever walked down it. And that morning I walked her and sitting there, on a ledge, in very plain sight, was a deck of playing cards. I didn't connect the random cards to him until it was all over, but, looking back, I know now that he was watching me. How else would a fresh deck of cards end up on a secluded residential road?

The police came, took a report, and set out to find him, leaving me and my husband Noah alone, glued to our security monitor while we googled "gated neighborhoods in Los Angeles." Then we saw the prices and googled "how to train a small rescue dog to bite a groin."

About a half hour later, ICK hadn't showed up and the nutjob rang my doorbell *again*. I quickly called the police *back* and they responded immediately, apprehending him a mere ten feet from my house, where he was lying on the ground in the dark, waiting. Thank God I never went outside to check where ICK was. After the police had arrested him and it was all over, an ICK "guard" finally showed up. We had initially called ICK at 11:14 P.M., and they came at 12:48 A.M. . . . That's a full hour and a half later. The woman arrived confused, said she had no idea what our call was about, had no information, and had only just been recently dispatched to come over. We told her what we had dealt with all night and that we probably had to cancel ICK because of it. She simply said "Yeah, no, I get it. I don't blame you." And she left. We called ICK the next day, relayed the entire story I just told you, and they immediately allowed us to cancel. So easy! And all it took was my stalker showing up to my house! I now have a different security company that's way more efficient: I just pay an angry German Shepherd in chicken nuggets to patrol the perimeter of my house.

While we're at it, you know what's kind of a scam? Restraining orders. If somebody is insane or on drugs or really wants to hurt you, they are going to. Don't you think that if they possessed the emotional intelligence to adhere to rules then maybe they wouldn't be trying to hurt you in the first place? Restraining orders are mostly there so that if and when someone attempts to harm you *again*, you have a clearer path to *maybe* having them be arrested or *maybe* going to prison.

> A restraining order is also extremely difficult to obtain. You basically have to be already dead to prove someone was trying to kill you. I had a written statement from the LAPD after my stalker had intermittently harassed me for years. Starting with him coming to a show, then by tagging me online and writing a (since-deleted) rambling post about killing people, then by showing up to my house the first time, then the second time. But due to some random clerical error, the detective I worked

with hadn't printed his signed statement on LAPD letterhead, and the judge read it and flippantly said, "I don't know who this letter is from," and wanted to dismiss my entire case. Over that detail.

By the grace of GOD, the detective happened to be in the building when I called him, and he came to the courtroom and testified. Had he not? I wouldn't have been granted a temporary restraining order that day. I needed to have that piece of paper as protection because he never went to prison. He was merely being held in jail until his day in court. And when that day came, the judge decided that rather than send him back to his home state, the state he took a bus from for the explicit purpose of finding my house and stalking me, it would be best to *keep* him in LA in a program that my taxes pay for. He would get to be monitored here, put down roots here, and make a life and friends here, in my city. He would, of course, be allowed out and about during the day and would have to check in with someone at night, but if he goes nuts during the day? I just need to *hope* they find him before something happens.

To this day I've never met this stalker or spoken to him, but one thing is for certain: When he "completes treatment," he will be a resident in my city and I get to look over my shoulder the rest of my life. I have deep paranoia about him finding me. I have a legitimate fear of sitting alone in my own backyard. I try not to think about it too much because I don't want to manifest it into reality. But I can't help it. I'd be stupid to just "get over it." And I only wrote about it here because I'm sure there are plenty of people who have to deal with the same bullshit.

Look, the guy is clearly unstable. I don't think prison is right for him, but I also don't think him being allowed to stay in LA is right either. Send him back to his home state; at least give us some distance. Maybe don't make it easier for him to have access to me?

I wanted a permanent restraining order so badly so I would have some insurance in case he came back, as I have been advised that these types of people frequently do. I mean, I post my local set times every week; I'm not hard to find.

I was only recently granted a restraining order, and it's only because I was able to consistently show up in court, file papers, and keep tabs on this.

I sat in the hallway of the courthouse, and I looked at all the people who were there trying to get restraining orders on just that day alone. I took stock of the demographic waiting, for many of whom English wasn't their first language and many of whom were women dealing with a domestic abuse case, meaning they were trying to get protection from someone they lived with. I just remember thinking, *Oh my God, if someone fills out one of these ten forms (in triplicate) wrong or doesn't have someone backing them up, they just have to go home and live with the person harassing them*. I thought, *What if you have a real job and you can't just take off work to sit and wait in a courtroom all day? What if your husband is beating you and it's your word against his* and *you have kids?* You just have to hope the father of your children doesn't murder you in your own home? And if you survive that, you have to hope you don't lose your job while you wait endlessly in the halls of a courthouse? Especially living in a city like Los Angeles, where the social divides are so disparate, I always think about how if something is this awful for me, it must feel insurmountably impossible for someone who doesn't have access to my resources or privilege.

Most expiration dates are a scam.

You know what usually tells you that food is expired? The food. You've never had bad milk and thought, *That was delicious and tangy and lumpy and—oops, it's five weeks old!* You've never looked at green meat that smelled like dog mouth and thought, *I'm gonna enjoy every bite of this furry beef.*

> Ever been to Europe? Food is just OUT. It's on counters as *cicchetti*, out on bars as tapas. Meat is out. Cheese is out. Markets are open. Ever been to an outdoor market in Asia? In the Middle East? Dead animals are piled; baked goods are stacked. Food is out and touching the air and people *aren't* dying from it. Everything in the US is hermetically sealed and preserved in chemicals and plastic and we are the fattest, sickest country. Only in America could a network have a show and multiple spin-offs all centered around the world of people so morbidly obese, they physically cannot get out of bed.

Part of the explanation for expiration dates, I believe, has to do with corporate liability and the exploitative and litigious nature of many Americans. Ah, America, land of the lawsuit. "I drank a gallon of year-old hot yogurt because no one explicitly told me *not* to, give me a billion dollars, I'm a moron and it's someone else's fault and it's my GOD-GIVEN constitutional right to be an idiot and profit off it." If a company can err on the safe side and print a label telling you their eggs expire a week from purchase instead of going to court over your claimed foodborne illness, they will. The sentiment seems to be: Who cares if we waste food, as long as massive corporations save some money because people can't be trusted to trust their own mouths and eyes? Plus, if the consumer has to throw it out faster, that means they have to buy more, faster. The planet should be okay . . .

In terms of legislation, of course we need laws about corporate liability, but we also need laws about people not being fucking idiots.

> But yeah, a cold case in most countries is just for items that *need* to be cold, like ice cream, not literally everything regardless of ideal temperature. You don't really need to have a plastic-wrapped pastry *in* a refrigerated case, yet we do it. Probably because some moron sued a gas station because he ate a room-temperature danish and then got cancer a year later and decided the two were connected.

Another thing that's a scam?

Public-facing altruism.

Doing kind things in the public eye hoping to garner pure adoration is exhausting and often doesn't yield the mass admiration from others for which you were hoping. Here's why: People hate people who try. It makes them feel insecure about their own lack of activism or initiative, or it makes them feel that the way they are doing something is wrong even though your actions have nothing to do with them. You will always be faulted for not doing "enough," whatever "enough" means on that day to whatever random person is hate-watching you on the Internet from their toilet. I've heard things like, "Why don't you donate your salary?" when I've posted a link to a charity. I opened my book with this, but it bears repeating. The endless sophistry of "Why are you trying to do anything when you've done something flawed in the past?," the "Why are you promoting saving the turtles when you have a car that runs on gas?"

is the counterproductive but deafening battle cry of the helpless and the angry, and it wrecks positive actions and goodwill. Because when someone publicly calls you out for trying to do something, their goal is rarely to help you. Their goal is to expose your flaws and undermine your entire action . . . and then eat your face.

Public approval is an ever-moving target. Whatever kind act you demonstrate can easily be waved off by pointing out the myriad things you didn't do. If you were to release a statement saying how much you give and to whom, you only leave yourself open to "Why wasn't it more? Why wasn't it a different charity? Why are you showing this off, you self-aggrandizing asshole?"

Years ago, my husband and I were in San Francisco, and we waited in line at Tartine, a tasty bakery. While waiting in line, I started doing a hamster voice and saying, "It's Tartine" over and over. Try it; it's so satisfying. I thought it would be so adorable if a little hamster came out of the kitchen holding a box of cookies, offering them around. "Tartine? It's Tartine. Do you know Tartine?" So I made a cute little Instagram video of me walking around, offering our box of pastries to imaginary people off camera in that voice. "Tartine? Say it's Tartine. Tartine? Is that you?" If you were familiar with me before purchasing this book, then that story is very on brand. If you weren't, well . . . Tartine!

We overordered, and, not wanting to throw the extra food away before heading to the airport, I decided to give some of the pastries to a homeless person. We did not film that because it's gross to film yourself being a good person. I even think it's gross that I'm telling you I did that, but I need you to know it for context. But yes, it is weird to let people know a small good thing you did. It just is. The ego weirdly offsets the intention. Anyway, one of the first comments I got on the fake-hamster-voice Tartine video was "why wouldn't you just give it to a homeless person. SMH."

I've always wanted to have the kind of money where I could leave a life-changing tip for a waiter.

Regardless of mediocre service, I believe you should always tip 20 percent. If the guy is deliberately a dick and kicks salad at you and slaps your baby, then you can reevaluate. But here is why you should always tip. If the waiter is bad, you *not* tipping isn't going to make them stop, think, reevaluate their performance and how they can be better and then go do better. They're not gonna "look inward" and think that they were the problem. No, they're just going to think you're a jerk and continue being subpar. Tipping, whether you like the economic model of it or not, is part of the agreement when you dine out in the United States. The waiter makes almost no money, probably has no health insurance, and *depends* on tips. You have the money to eat out and tacitly entered into this financial arrangement when you walked in. It's not a performance review; it's part of what you owe for services rendered. My husband is a chef and often (too often?) talks about how we should do away with tipping entirely and just charge more for the food and pay people a liveable wage. But instead we do tipping.

I've always wanted to be famous enough that if I left a big tip, it made the news. Not like global Al Jazeera news, but, like, clickbait pop-up news. And the waitress would post the receipt where I left a hundred thousand dollars and be interviewed and say, "She was just so humble and effortlessly gorgeous. It wasn't until she left that we realized who that anonymous

STUNNING woman was. Even under her jacket you could tell she was so toned."

The headline would read something *sensational* like, "Comedian Iliza Shlesinger leaves LIFE-CHANGING tip in Joliet, IL, Steak 'n Shake." Something sexy like that, and Shlesinger would be spelled correctly! And I've for sure done it a few times, left a large tip. It feels good to do it in a small town for a waiter who was super friendly or overworked. But no one has ever posted about it. Not once. I did, however, one time preemptively check out of a hotel because it wasn't great, and I got tagged in a RAGE post from the front desk worker telling everyone I was a huge bitch. Weird that she had that much to say since my husband was the one who checked us out while I took the dog for a walk.

Many, many mom-focused products are a scam.

Just because you become a mother doesn't mean you lose all sense of style and reality. You may be preoccupied, you may have rearranged your priorities, and you may not be a Party Goblin who owns the night anymore, but you don't automatically downgrade to gullible idiot just because you had a child.

After years of trying to adopt, a friend of mine finally got a baby girl. I wanted to get her a "new mom" gift basket. I didn't want to get her a flammable, cheap diaper tower or something to keep the baby safe, like a BB gun. I wanted to get her cool new-mom stuff and, since she had adopted, I didn't need to get her birth recovery items like "NIPPLE SALVE" "PERINEUM CBD BALM," or "A VAGINA BATHROBE."

I just wanted to get her something chic with items that would make her feel special, and I wanted an Instagram-based, modern, Millennial-focused, ultra-cool mommy company who labels in FUTURA FONT to tell me what those things should be.

You know how there are cool accounts for cool moms by cool moms? It's always a maternity company started by a mom named Serabella who wears straw hats indoors and has three children named Chicory, Skyh, and a baby who's just named the letter H. She curates the best in hot mommy care for her account. An account that shows a diverse array of moms taking empowering photos in nursing bras, proudly displaying their stretch marks (that they call Tiger Stripes, what a fun rebrand!), laughing over a cup of cucumber tea, their smiles belying the horrors of childbirth. A cool company that sells cozy mommy sweat sets . . . in oatmeal! I thought, *These ladies will definitely have an angle on this! The gift box will be filled with handcrafted de-stress moisturizing masks and precharged crystals and your own personal bumblebee to make wax for your upper lip and eco-friendly puke towels.* That's what I wanted. I wanted that account that I made up. So I clicked around and I found a facsimile of my fantasy. I looked into their new-mom gift baskets.

The basket included . . .

A scarf:

A fucking scarf. My first thought was that this company bulk-ordered them for something else and couldn't get rid of them so pivoted and tried to make it a "mommy scarf," selling you on the idea that there are scarves specifically for women who have children, which are very different from normal scarves for childless women.

"Great for dressing up a look or just keeping Mama warm while she's out conquering the world!" The fact that they wrote a blurb about why a human would need a *scarf* at all, to me, further proves how dumb we think women are. As if there is some tired mom out there typing into Google "What is scarf and how?" "Neck cold, how do I hot it?"

When I say "we," I am referring to society, copyrights, companies, and overall general opinion. I'm in no way taking personal responsibility. We/they market to women like they are giant toddlers. This endless pejorative female-targeted infantilization of the English language when it's directed toward women:

"Mama Bear needs her beauty rest!"

"Rock-star gal gets her glam on!"

"Werk it, she-ntrepreneur!"

"Be a divalicious ass kicker in stilettos!"

"The biggest badass boss babe in *her*story."

"The fiercest *she-matologist* working in the blood lab!"

This pervasive rhetoric is basically watered-down, digestible empowerment designed to get a woman's money. It's the advertising equivalent of a LIVE LAUGH LOVE sign.

You know what feminism *isn't*? It isn't calling history "herstory." Men are never going to adopt it; it will never be in the history books or a dictionary. That is because history has nothing to do with the word "his"; it has nothing to do with the idea that it is *his*, meaning a man's story. History is taken from the Greek word "historia," meaning the act of seeking knowledge. You wanna make history more about women? Start by electing more of them and shining lights on our historically minimized contributions. And, if you must engage in word play? Start by writing it as "hystory" because the Latin "hysteria" means "from the womb." I know, "herstory" is supposed to be a cheeky jab at the patriarchy, but it's tolerated, never preferred. Make real arguments and real points to further an agenda; don't clog up my feed with sophomoric faux-empowerment. Quit covering all my products in glitter; it's bad for the environment and I'm not twelve.

Anyway, the scarf was offensively dumb. No new mom is lactating, in pain, exhausted, and wringing her hands, yelling, "IF ONLY I HAD A SCARF TO TIE THIS LOOK TOGETHER!"

Lip gloss:

Not balm, gloss. Not ChapStick. Gloss. So it's not about moisturizing, it's about wet lips, and they sell it to you with that bullshit femme-centric jargon again, like, "Keeping Mama's lips looking hot on the go!" Yes, that's every mother's priority, making sure strangers think her lips are wet like a shiny, juicy vagina while shame-feeding her baby in a closet at work on her break!

A wine tumbler/wineglass:

They always have something on it like *the queen's cup* or *this is water* or *mommy's vacation in a glass*. I really resent the idea that a woman would even need to conceal having a fucking GLASS OF WINE while parenting. I think it's much more about our society's judgment of women relaxing and our constant scrutiny of any mother's actions than it is playful. I don't see a lot of beer glasses geared toward men that say **DAD GAS** or **PAPA MILK**.

Reusable water bottle:

"Rock-star mama bear bitch gets thirstayyyy SLAYIN' and kickin' butt!"

> We have to stop. We have to stop thinking MASS-producing plastic, metal, latex-encased reusable water bottles is helping the planet. If we issued one to every person, then fine. But I have about ten of these that have been forced on me as promotional gifts or regular gifts. "I heard you were a fan of our planet; here's something that saves it in theory but not in practice." "Our company cares about the planet; here's our logo emblazoned into metal to prove we care. We also included some stickers and a

T-shirt and a hat! Go green! It says it right here on this plastic keychain! But hey, you can try to recycle the packaging we over-packed it with. Thanks for taking care of our mess!"

You really only need ONE reusable water bottle. They are made to last forever. The ubiquity of these is scary. Like the straw thing. People heard plastic was bad (which it is) and just started, instead, making or buying metal straws en masse. Good swap, right? Because metal is super easy to forge, takes no energy to mold, and is so light to ship . . . I put that in the same category as reusable totes. Great, have a few for groceries. But we got rid of plastic and replaced it with . . . cotton totes. Cotton, which takes water to grow, energy to harvest and make. Humans are decent at reusing if it's convenient; we really struggle with reducing, and recycling is hard and, sadly, in many cities, doesn't actually happen on a large enough scale to put a dent in the damage being done.

Anyway, I opted out of the mom gift basket. I think I just gave her an envelope of money instead—I don't remember. But I thought about it, and my association with lame gifts in relation to mothers started before I had searched for that gift set. I've always struggled with getting my own mother a gift. If the average person wants to get their mother something other than (overpriced) flowers on Mother's Day, what are the immediate options? "Oh, do you want an ugly Hummelesque of a mama rabbit holding her baby rabbit? Do you want a fifteen-dollar silver-plated necklace of a rose framing a heart holding a plaque that says A MOTHER'S LOVE? A coffee mug that says "BOW TO THE QUEEN"? She's seventy-two; she has been drinking coffee for fifty years; she has mugs. Skin care? Again, she's seventy-two—she has her own routine. A candle from your col-lection? Have fun guessing *which* brand of "summer breeze" won't be nauseating. And if she doesn't love it, you get to watch that candle collect dust every time you stay in your parents' guest room.

iTunes:

Once seen as not a scam but, in fact, the cheap new way to buy music and the easiest way to listen to all the hits, iTunes had its run then was soon replaced with streaming music/subscription services, and we realized we don't need to "own" music because it's always available and ever streaming. So iTunes as a concept isn't a scam, but iTunes is on this list because, like your Apple ID, it will follow you forever. For the rest of my life, if I open a random audio file it opens up my iTunes on my computer, an app I can't seem to get rid of. Every time I open an MP3 I have to reckon with the one Akon song I bought in 2010 and season two of *Whale Wars*.

Curiosity on the Internet is a scam.

I know, I sound like a conspiracy theorist edgelord. Here's the flaw in a practical application of "the algorithm" of social media that runs our lives. I go online and search for "gray sweatpants." Maybe I use Instagram.

> Doesn't it seem like thousands of clothing brands popped up overnight? Brands I've never heard of describe their garments with phrases like "our *classic* vintage tee," "buttery soft vegan cotton, back by popular demand," "our most popular fit yet," and I'm thinking *How do you have a classic T-shirt when your brand is only three years old? What makes it popular? That thirty people bought it in a flash sale?* It's a scam. I bet it all comes from the same fast-fashion factory making all your other clothes.

So I find and buy sweatpants. But now the Internet knows I bought them. They're onto me! I have to endure pop-ups for MORE

SWEATPANTS! How is that helpful? Advertise to me in a few years! Why show me ads for the same thing at the same time I bought the thing?

Merely existing means enduring a ceaseless barrage of e-newsletters, e-updates, pop-up ads, and having company flyers jammed into every crevice of your windshield, front door, and mailbox.

> And yes, I know I'm supposed to be hypervigilant about my own cybersecurity, but honestly, I don't care that you've updated your terms and conditions. I didn't even know what they were when I bought a (SINGULAR) USB cord from your website two years ago.

Any email coming from a company I've shopped with does nothing to entice me. If one shows up in my email, it's on a fast track to my SPAM/BLOCK filter. If you bother me, I will wield the little power I have as a consumer, and I will never shop with you again.

You would think a company wouldn't want to be tuned out, so they would space out their "thanks for your purchase, be back in six minutes with a 5 percent off coupon you have to use in the next four minutes!" emails. You would think companies wouldn't want to offend you by sending you pop-up ads for weight-loss surgery because you googled "healthy breakfast." But they don't care; it's all about data collection, brand recognition, the power of suggestion, and casting the widest net possible as often as possible until someone gives in.

I believe the ever-watching eye of the algorithm kills curiosity.

"You like cute, fuzzy chicks?"

YES! CLICK!

"Any other farm animals? Baby cows?"

Yes. So cute. Click. Click.
"What about a baby cow with mama cow?"
YES!
"Baby cow being ripped away from Mama?!"
Oh no!
"Baby cow being slaughtered in front of Mama!"
NO!

> Now you've seen a cow homicide and you're sitting at your desk crying because you can't unsee it and no matter how much meat you don't eat, it's not enough to make a real impact on our planet. You're depressed and you need a pick-me-up, so you do a little Internet shopping . . . Oh, look, sweatpants!

You can no longer be a voyeur because merely looking is, in and of itself, an interaction. You are brought into the equation that feeds it.

> If you don't look, things go away. That's how TV ratings work. That's how popularity works. If enough people don't watch, don't subscribe, and don't give something attention, then it goes away. It's the reason you close your eyes tight when you think there's a monster in your room. If you don't look at it, it's not real to you. But now I can't even look out of curiosity, because the Internet can't tell the difference between gawking and genuine interest. You looked and they saw you look.

I can't click on a weird pair of ugly shoes to get a better look, hate-scroll through someone's account, or even just click on a juicy C-list celebrity headline because that tells THE INTERNET that I clicked, which, to them, means I care. CLICKING = CARING!

The Internet decides what you care about, and it becomes your world. I once clicked on a "motivational speaker" (with clearly a bunch of purchased followers. He had two million followers and only about fifty views per post, so . . .). It was a lot of cheesy videos of him working out while quoting the Bible. I clicked because there was a typo in one of his posts about "Strifing for your goals" and I thought it was a joke account—it wasn't. For the next three weeks my feed was peppered with this guy, his idiot friends, and "similar" accounts of half-wits in tight three-piece suits spouting aphorisms about challenge and perseverance . . . and lateral reps. In fact, if you're listening to this book out loud as an audiobook . . . your phone just heard all of those key words. So good luck.

Dear Internet: You want my info? Take it. Take my fucking five Beyoncé songs I bought on iTunes and my date of birth and left-blank professional field on my Facebook page I never check. I am silently fighting you. That's right, I go to great lengths to keep my algorithm filled with relevant things, and you aren't going to gunk it up!

> I created an account to cringe-watch people. I don't hate-watch. I don't watch people I "hate"—I just peer at people who I can't believe are real. Everyday idiots I used to be friends with, people I'm jealous of, and celebrities I wish I was dumb enough to look up to. I made up a fake name and a fake email so I could have a garbage profile that has all the dumb celebrity gossip, people who annoy me whom I can't stop looking at, and tenuous conspiracy theory videos I don't want inundating me during the day but like to treat myself by watching after a long week. I never interact with them; I never comment or like anything. I don't interfere with their lives, and all I ask in return is that they don't interfere with mine by popping up, uninvited, to my real

feed. My fake account is to my real account what a cheater's apartment is to his real house with his wife and kids. I do things with my fake account I could never do with my real account.

Constantly upgrading technology is a scam.

It's a weird guarantee that almost anything you buy is going to break, will arrive incomplete, parts will be missing, will require you purchase more space, dongles will be lost. Parts will be out of warranty. Technicians will be unreachable. Sizes will not be what you thought they were. And one thing is for sure, if a company is big enough, they don't care if they let you down. Weirdly, for as disliked as Amazon is, they make returns easy. You don't feel like a criminal when you report something missing or broken; they reach their reptilian claw into their money volcano, and they say, "Here's a refund."

Airlines treat you like a hostage, cable companies treat you like a liar, and cell phone companies force you into a feudal lord system.

Now, I don't want to use this book to put people on blast and look victimized or virtuous. I didn't want to vilify the major cell phone company worker who tried to ruin my life . . .

That's a lie. Yes, I do. And since Sprint was absorbed by T-Mobile, I can go ahead and tell you it was Sprint. A few years ago, my husband and I went to the Sprint store to upgrade our phones. We don't upgrade often, maybe once every four years? If my phone lets me check email and Instagram incessantly, then I don't need the technology for it to double as a robot butler. It was about four thirty; the store closed at six. I know this because the overworked middle-management hamster in a yellow polo shirt helping us specifically said we had gotten there just in the nick of time to get all of the information on our phones transferred over to the new phones. I remember him saying, "Had you gotten here a few minutes from now, we couldn't do it. But we can get it done in time." I was so happy we were able to knock this errand out because I had just had a procedure done on my eyeballs and for the next two days my eyesight, while adjusting, would vacillate between *extreme* nearsightedness and *extreme* farsightedness. That day was a nearsighted day. I could see shapes, but I couldn't read. I would have to hold something up to basically the bridge of my nose to make out what it said, like Monstro staring at Pinocchio through a hole. So, he said the phones would be ready at six P.M. Perfect, just enough time for Noah to take me home so I could "rest my eyes" and he'd come back for our phones. Noah dropped me at home and called me around five forty-five. "The guy says the phones aren't ready." I said, "Okay, whatever, we can just get them tomorrow." "He won't do that, and he says we can't leave them here overnight . . ."

To this day I wonder if that's like corporate policy or just something the guy made up. I said, "Well, he made a really big deal about how we had gotten there just in time; he won't stay and let it all transfer over?" He wouldn't. "And can we just put everything back on the old phone and come back tomorrow?" No, he wouldn't do that either.

He said he had already erased the old phones and all the information was somewhere in the air, between the phones. Either I could have my old phone back, totally empty, or I'd have to take the new phone and just be happy with whatever data had made it over so far.

Did I believe him? Not really. Does it seem like a company that sells new phones would be more adept at transferring information? Yes. Was he closing the store and forcing us out? Yep.

I was so sad. I had my first texts with my husband on that phone, our first pictures, family pictures, life events. I had JOKES WRITTEN DOWN. All of it, gone. And this is where you can say, "You should have used the cloud to back it up." But I have been the victim of an iCloud hack, and if you've ever had personal information stolen, it will shake your faith in e-security. I appreciate that I could be backing up my life on my computer (does anyone really do that?) but it shouldn't matter. This guy shouldn't have the power to erase my memories because he felt like playing Phone God. Then I thought, *Two can play at that game.* I'm gonna make this not about him but about the shitty massive company he works for. Nothing wrong with going after a multimillion-dollar corporate goliath who doesn't care about their customers.

I took to Twitter. Twitter: The Only Choice When You Want to Shame a Corporation Publicly and Be Supported by Misanthropes with Whom You Otherwise Wouldn't Engage. I typed at one hundred miles per hour, holding the phone up to my eyeball, hoping it was all coming out typo-free. I tagged the phone company over and over like a maniac, detailing my story until someone from the company contacted me. The Sprint employee even made a brand-new Twitter account just to harass me on that thread; it was Thunderdome in 140-character spurts. In the end, Sprint, horrified at this employee's weird vigilante rule making, ended up just letting us have our new phones for free. We agreed to keep our service with the company (not out of good faith; they are just, weirdly, the only cell company that works in our area), and we all moved on.

You can file that story however you would like. You can say they only cared because I had followers, but I can't respect rules randomly gerrymandered by an employee in a bad mood. If I'm having a bad day, I don't do twenty minutes of material and then just stare at the audience for another forty minutes and fart; I do my job. And I don't believe, rich or poor, that, if you can help it, you should ever have to stand for someone deciding how your life is going to go based on their feelings. I believe you should always use your voice, and I believe you should treat every person you meet like they have the power to go fully insane and launch a thirty-tweet rant thread about you that the whole world will see. Just be cool and respect my money, and I won't have a problem with you.

The counterpoint to my list of scams could be that if scams ceased to exist, our society would perhaps cease to function because scams are part of a free market, an integral part of capitalism. And with a sucker born every minute, why wouldn't you want to try and take their money? And now that I've elucidated the reality of the *Matrix* situation we live in, may God grant you the money, energy, and time to opt out of all this bullshit.

WHERE HAVE ALL THE HOT BOYS GONE?

Here is what I remember the most about being a teenager. You ready? Okay, here it goes. I remember . . .

Being super horny.

I hate that word, but it's apt. I remember there being such a desire to be with (re: make out with) a boy but no *real* way to do it. Especially if you live in the suburbs, like, where are you supposed to meet boys? If you live in a city, you can *walk* to the corner store or take public transit or be next to one on a crowded street. But for the rest of the country, the options are limited. Of course, now there is the Internet, and I hate to be the one to say this, but I need to make this clear to my younger readers, my teenage readers and people who think it's normal to fall in love with someone they've never met. A relationship on the Internet isn't the same as in real life. I know, that's upsetting.

If you're fourteen, you go to school and then you go home. You might have some time after school before your mom gets home, but that limits you to boys in walking distance, which, if you go to public school in a suburb or a rural area, are the kids you go to school with, so it's not very adventurous. Options are limited.

When I was in middle school in Plano, Texas, there was a kid in my class named Travis. It was Texas in the nineties, there were a lot of kids named Travis. But *my* Travis was the kind of kid who would be a dad at fifteen.

I thought he was so cute. I knew three things about him.

1. He sometimes was on my bus home.
2. He lived in one of the apartment complexes behind my house.
3. And he wore JNCOs.

I pined for him, listening to "Why I Love You So Much" by Monica. I think we had two conversations ever. It was a deep love.

When we were like thirteen to fifteen, and wanted to talk to boys outside of school? The best bets for communing with the opposite sex were . . .

- Hoping your girlfriend had a cute brother who was somehow age-appropriate, which meant, basically, exactly your age. At thirteen or fourteen, girls are more mature than boys, and no one wants to kiss a twelve-year-old, and a boy who's sixteen is basically middle-aged compared to a thirteen-year-old. So a hot brother who is the same age as your friend, so basically a twin. Which is weird.

But yeah, a friend having a brother who was cute and normal. A non-pervert cute brother who was age-appropriate. Not some weird nineteen-year-old half brother who was on parole and lived in the guesthouse.

- Hoping your girlfriend had parents who let them have boys over. THAT was the best. Parents who would allow their daughters to have teenage boys over and "let the kids have the upstairs for the night."

> That's what you want to look for: a friend whose mom is on their second marriage to a guy named Don—maybe they met at a Martini Blues, maybe Don never does the top two buttons on his short-sleeved Tommy Bahama shirts, maybe Don has a daughter from another lifetime who's like twenty-seven and waitresses in San Diego. But that's what you want, as a teenager, is to be friends with the girl whose parents see their kid having a sleepover as their opportunity to also have their adult friends over so they can get loose. While you're ordering pizza, they're drinking full-bodied Cabs out of glasses with wine charms, and the moms wear sleeveless turtleneck bodysuits with big zippers up the front from Caché. You're in the den playing spin the bottle with an empty can of Surge and you know the parents are in the garage-turned-Don's-rumpus-room swinging with their weird friends. (Well, you didn't actually know then, but you know now.) It's the perfect deal: Everyone gets to have a sexual experience from the comfort of a Berber-carpeted room with their shoes off.

• Going somewhere unsupervised, like a water park or a Six Flags. Whole relationships formed, flourished, and ended within the confines of amusement parks. You have *hours* to meet guys from exotic places like whatever city is over forty-five minutes from your house or, ooooh, other school districts! You could flirt, bond in a two-hour line for the log flume, and then spend the whole day soaked in theme-park-river water, thigh skin chafing in your wet jean shorts, still trying to flirt while your arms and face turned Yosemite Sam mustache red in the sun. At the end of the day you'd exchange numbers and then never see each other again.

But cute boys weren't just *out*—you had to hunt them down. Like truffles. (Did you laugh at that? That makes you the truffle pig, ladies!) But cute boys weren't where girls were. I remember playing sports next to a field of boys' sports just HOPING one would catch me running in slow motion, like the movies had promised.

Girls would go to the mall, but usually the boys weren't there. Because, nineties stand-up premise forthcoming . . . BECAUSE MEN HATE shopping. Yes, malls were, historically, where kids went to hang out, but it was usually guys who you didn't want to date. Like, cool, if you're attracted to the teen gang loitering in front of the Lids or the slightly older guy hanging out while his friend ran the register at PacSun.

The moments of being alone with a boy were so excruciatingly precious. Your parents were trying to protect you, but the curfew was always too fucking early. I JUST NEED SOME PRIVACY SO I CAN MAKE OUT IN PEACE AND TALK MY WAY OUT OF GIVING A HAND JOB! I LITERALLY JUST NEED FIVE MORE MINUTES!

Even as an adult, to spot a hot, available, and normal guy in the wild? RARE. They are simply just not out as frequently as the rest of us, who are strange or average-looking people. Just like you see a lot of pigeons every day, then you see, like, a bright red cardinal and you stop in your tracks. You whisper to your friend, "Oh my God, look! Look how pretty! Where did he come from?" That's how it feels to spot a stunning guy just out in the general population getting frozen yogurt, acting like a person. Why is it so rare?

Partly because the truth is that most people aren't attractive. But the other truth is that men have the agency to do more fun things solo than women do. They satisfy themselves. A lot of women make a big showing of "me time"; they let everyone know with an Instagram story post "I'M NOT DATING NOW, I'M JUST BEING WITH MYSELF. I'M TAKING MYSELF ON A HIKE TO GET TO KNOW ME!" then they repost a "Top Ten Ways to Let Go of Toxic Habits" Instagram story. Then post a lot of pictures of them alone to show how they are thriving being alone.

For the most part, men just go. They don't post a bulletin; they don't tell their guy friends they need to reflect and "spiritually detox." No, you won't know an attractive, aloof guy was taking time for himself until you haven't been able to reach him all weekend and thought he was dead. Then he texts you back a week later to tell you he "just wanted to get away, and so I headed to the woods for a bit, didn't have to think about letting anyone know in case someone tried to rape me in the woods, because I'm a dude and I can move through this world with impunity."

> Have you ever been to Denver? I'm not sure how that city has businesses because everyone is always outside having fun.
> California is the same way. Think about it: You know a lot more men than you realize who are just "in the desert for the weekend." or "up in Big Bear for the week, working remotely. Alone. No one to hear my screams."

It's incredible that men and women meet each other at all given how different their interests are.

Hot men deliberately hunt. They are not just *out*. I worked on a show with a VERY handsome executive who told me that he goes to bed at eight thirty. Eight thirty! P.M.! What good is looking rested if no one is seeing it?! "Sex was great; can you shut the blinds? I want to be asleep before dusk." He would go to bed early so he could get up early every morning to surf. I think he was secretly dating a dolphin. Or another surfer. Or no one and just loved surfing.

Oftentimes women are told that dating is about quantity over quality, the idea being that if you go out with enough guys, the buckshot approach to dating, eventually you'll get one you like.

> Part of that is due to society's insistence that you, as a beautiful woman, should "just give him a shot" even if you are repulsed by him physically. We tend to not urge men to give a shot or a second attempt with a girl they aren't attracted to simply because "she's really nice and maybe you will become attracted to her." You see it in movies all the time. If a woman loves a hot guy in the first act, the rest of the movie has to then reveal her being shown that who she *really* loves in the less attractive guy who was kind all along. The male equivalent of this in movies is the guy just learns to love a brunette instead of a blonde.

With all that said, I want to share my wealth of knowledge from my journey as a single woman.

PLACES TO FIND HOT MEN

- On mountains
  * They are always "headed to the mountains" with their dog, who is always named Bailey, or a gargoyle of a dog named Bella. She's a rescue lab/pit mix with a butt breath and dirty, knobby elbows but you gotta go through her to get to him.

- Military bases
- Comedy shows
- Sports bars and gritty Irish bars
- Opening weekends of *Mission: Impossible* and Jason Bourne movies

PLACES HOT MEN ARE NOT
- Brunch
- Pilates
- Singles events
- Nail places
- Group fitness classes that don't involve flipping tires or an Australian theme
- Anything having to do with wine at a lower price point
- Any bar with good dancing
- Literally anywhere you are when you are single

When you're a teenager, you have tons of hormones just coursing through your perfect body. This is why teenagers are horny, stupid, and irrational. It's also why they fall in love so easily and so hard. Then, as we get older, women experience societal pressure/a desire to fertilize an egg, which is why we (or, at least, a lot of us) seek out stability, marriage, and having children. It's all in our biochemistry. Men don't have that same pressure. Ask a thirty-five-year-old woman about her goals and, business aside, I think you'll often hear, "To be happy. Maybe have a family, to find the right person." What you never hear a woman say is, "To be fully realized, to defy my own mortality. To get my body fat to −1 percent, and biohack my theta waves to optimize my sleep. To hold my breath in arctic waters for over an hour. To fist fight a puma. To harvest my own supply of adrenochrome. To shrug and have the world crumble. And in the meantime? Just keep on fuckin' for fun." Anyway, even if you're smart, you're never dumber than when you are young.

It was the last night of camp, and I was fourteen. I know I was fourteen because *Men in Black* had just come out, and I remember the boy I had been flirting with all summer did a talent-show dance to the *Men in Black* theme song. That's right, he did a talent-show dance to the *MIB* theme song, and it wasn't a turnoff. That's where your attraction radar is at fourteen. But even at camp, without your parents and with miles of wooded areas, your sensual alone time is relegated to that one free hour after dinner or maybe thirty minutes before lights-out. But it was the last night of camp, so there was a repercussion-less/*Purge* kind of vibe in the air.

I attended summer camp in upstate New York, and summers in upstate New York are chilly at night and in the morning—pretty exotic to me, a girl from Texas. I was just used to HEAT from sunup to sundown for eight months straight. In Texas, if it's anytime between January and October and the sun is out? It's gonna get ya. So the chance to wear a sweatshirt to breakfast, at camp, was a unique one! Which is great because at fourteen you desperately want to wear a hoodie that lets everyone know you have the sophisticated taste of, say, a seventeen-year-old. Something that says SEÑOR FROG'S or TARHEELS, something that shows you've heard of grown-up things and intend to participate in them as soon as you can drive. My mom was a good sport about getting me a Notre Dame sweatshirt for Hanukkah when I was thirteen. I didn't even know where the school was. I still don't.

His name was Dan. He was tall, thin, and had a soft voice. More important, he was cute and into me, which, I mean, what more does a girl need?

He and I stole away to one of the camp's theaters. It was a wooden structure, a theater-in-the-round. I remember it had no doors; it was like a pavilion. So we just wandered in, both ready to be caught and explain it away with the brilliant lie of "Oh, we were just gonna hang out in the doorway and talk." We found a couch with a tarp over it under the bleachers. A secluded bed-like structure with a privacy flap is all a teenager could ever want; it's all most rent-paying twenty-year-olds in Manhattan could ever afford. And it was the first time I got to really *lie down* with a boy—how adult! How sophisticated! Up until then, most making out was done standing in a public space! But this was special: This was a ratty theater couch they'd repurposed for a production of *Pippin*; it was perfect. And we got to spend real time making out. Sex wasn't an option because, gosh, the only reason I can think is that I didn't want to? Because I was fourteen? I was "just there for the make out."

I carried that motto with me WELL into my thirties.

He lived in New Jersey and I lived in Texas, but we kept in touch. We would call each other late, after nine thirty P.M. CST. I just kept hoping my mom never said anything about the long-distance charges. It was 1997, and I had my own phone line. Looking back, I don't know why I wanted that—I wasn't taking that many calls, and I certainly had no pressing business. But he would call. I would hover over the phone, and in the split second it rang I would pick it up, praying my mother hadn't heard it across the house. I would pick up the receiver and whisper, "Hold on," then hold my breath, waiting to hear the distinctly heavy vibration of the heels of her bare feet coming toward me on the hallway tile. Truthfully, I don't think she ever came, but I still had that fear of waking her up and being found out. We talked all through that year, and I felt there was an actual chance "we" could "work." I knew I had a chance to see him because my mom would let me fly back east once a year to visit my camp friends around Christmas. She let me take this trip, *and* she gave me one hundred dollars to spend for the week I was in New York. One hundred dollars? All for a fourteen-year-old?! In New York City?! I was going to BUY THE BLOCK. I WAS A NO LIMIT SOLDIER! I was going to buy things, hang out with my friends, and see Dan, my fourteen-year-old soul mate.

I remember the desperation of wanting to see someone with no means of transportation. The desperation of wanting the freedom to be truly mobile makes up half of the pangs of adolescence. Wanting a car, wanting to drive it far, wanting to stay out. As an adult, these things are more burdens than anything else. The amount of nights I've sat in my home in Los Angeles (pre-baby) and thought, *I have money, a car, and access to alcohol yet I'm so bored and tired I just want to go to bed at eight so we can get to tomorrow and I can have another cup of coffee and complain about having to drive somewhere.*

Dan and I made a plan to meet in the city. He lived in southern New Jersey, which, coming from Texas, didn't seem *that* far from New York City. And it isn't, really, relative to how far I had come. I thought, *We took a train from Long Island to Manhattan. My dad used to take the train from Connecticut to Manhattan. Trains go everywhere here. Can't he just take the train into the city?* To a Dallasite, the fact that there was a train these kids back east could take to get to almost any state on the upper Eastern Seaboard blew my mind. Why couldn't he, at fourteen, take a series of trains and/or buses, alone, from Ocean City to Manhattan?! Everything seemed so close!

In 1997, my house in Texas backed up to a field! And behind that field was another field! Next to that was a massive toll road and then the Dallas city limits and then the city of Plano and then a bunch of nothing and then the state of Oklahoma. So I grew up on the edge of the suburbs of a major city but near the suburbs of a popular growing city. I lived on the edge of relevancy, the way I saw it. But I always felt a little more tied to something culturally relevant because I knew I had camp friends in New York. I would spend a few days on Long Island with one of them, and then someone's parents would drive me into the city, where I would meet up with the Manhattan camp friends and then meet up with Dan. And we had a plan!

Here was the perfect plan with no flaws: Once in New York City I was going to procure a fake ID without any knowledge of where to get one or what they cost. (Had any of this plan even come close to happening, I wouldn't have even had enough money because I would end up spending most of the hundred dollars on a shiny puffy *GOLD* Tommy Hilfiger *vest* and a Manhattan Portage messenger bag I got at a store run by a rat on St. Marks Place.) Back to the plan. I would find a store that would sell a fake ID to a fourteen-year-old that said she was eighteen. Then I was going to meet Dan at a courthouse (WHAT?!) with this fraudulent ID, *lie* to the government, have the government believe me, and then we were going to get married. MARRIED. I didn't even know my Social Security number. Why would I? I didn't even know how to give directions from the airport to my house! Then I would fly home. Married. Then enter the ninth grade.

The purpose of all of this? Wasn't even love. Wasn't even rebellion. It's just, well, probably the reason contraception should be free and available to all. Because even smart kids are dumb.

That was the flawless plan. That was our big idea.

My big idea. Sometimes my ideas are so vivid and fully realized in my own mind that I can't remember if I shared them. I have that problem to this day with arguments I fantasize about. I'll plan a whole argument and I'll tell my husband, "What I would say if . . ." and he'll listen, egging me on. "And then what would they say? And then what would you say?" And the conversation never actually happens, but it doesn't matter. In my mind, I won. In my mind, I was heard.

There were no cell phones really then. I certainly didn't have one. The biggest piece of electronics I owned was a Dell with an Intel Pentium II processor that I mostly used to play the CD-ROM of *You Don't Know Jack* (and sometimes I'd fiddle with that Zaurus). I got to Manhattan, and I called Dan from a pay phone. I was so nervous to see him again after all these months. All that buildup, all of that fantasizing. He answered. He couldn't come to the city, his mom said he had to do something with his family that day. And that was the end of that.

I went the rest of high school without talking to Dan. He wasn't at camp the next year, and without our red-hot love connection and plans of government/marital espionage, we fizzled out. One day in the early 2000s, well into my twenties, I got a Myspace message. It was Dan. We caught up, we chatted, there wasn't a *ton* to talk about since the only thing we ever really had in common was that we were attracted to each other and went to the same camp. And, of all the things, I was going to be in New York that month for a gig. Now, with our own money, cars, and apartments, there was nothing to stop us from seeing each other. Except I had a boyfriend. A boyfriend who I loved but who also thought I cheated on him all the time anyway, so we'll call it a self-fulfilling prophecy. We'll also call it me being like, twenty-four, and who cares? I really believe there isn't much you should have to apologize for in your twenties if no one died. He drove the hour to my hotel. To my surprise, he arrived with a friend. "He's here so I don't do anything stupid," Dan said. Maybe Dan had a girlfriend, I don't know. I think we kissed a few times, but it wasn't as magnetic as it once was. Nothing in your adult life will ever compare to the adolescent elation of camp kisses.

Weirdly, I still didn't want to sleep with him, and I didn't. Maybe it's that the *children* you're attracted to when you're fourteen don't hold the same raw sexual magnetism over a decade later. Maybe it was just the thrill of kissing someone I had frozen in my mind for all these years. Maybe it was just being BORED the night before a gig and a little curious. He left (with a boner—who cares?), and I flew home two days later. Eventually, I told my boyfriend what I did. We broke up and life moved on. I still think of Dan if I hear "Forget Me Nots" but never for any other reason, which is absolutely perfect.

MISCARRIAGE

As a society, we seem to be very interested in curbing women's reproductive rights while glossing over the negative potential outcomes of pregnancy. Because when it comes to women's reproductive health issues, we kind of just don't talk about it as much as we should for a topic that directly affects over three billion people. For example: One in eight women has had a miscarriage. It's something brutal that happens to so many women, yet you're probably unfamiliar with that statistic unless you've had one or know someone who has had one and you've discussed it. Then again, I kind of get it. Why would we know that? We all cringed in the early 2000s when "dead baby jokes" were a thing, so why talk about the nonfiction version? Moreover, why would anyone want to harp on something so miserable? Then again, our society is fascinated with death . . . and misery.

As a culture, we are obsessed with certain kinds of death. Female death, specifically if the woman is involved in something sexual (an affair), is sexual (a prostitute), or is a part of something deviantly sexual (a sex cult). We dedicate multi-season-long shows, miniseries, and documentaries to brutal deaths. *Law & Order: SVU*, a show that's only about sex crimes, sex murders, and sex-related death, has been on the air longer than some of the people read-ing this book have been alive (twenty-three years!). TV tackles female-specific issues from every angle: unwed pregnant women, rape, paternity tests, cougars, foster kids, teen moms, single moms, and adoption. But there is nothing about miscarriage, except for an occasional scene where a pregnancy that was unwanted in the first place is explained away by a character having lost the baby.

And if a show did focus on the topic, what would that show even be? A lithe girl fumbling her way down a New York City street while the narrator says, "Jessica Carriage wanted to have it all, but couldn't quite figure it out."

"This fall, Kaley Cuoco is . . . *Ms. Carriage.*"

We have whole book genres detailing women being sexually abused or going missing. I spend my nights perusing the synopses in the Amazon bookstore. So many thrillers for women start with:

"After her mother goes missing . . ."

"After her sister's disappearance . . ."

"When a hot woman disappears . . ."

"A woman's body is found . . ."

"A woman's body is missing . . ."

"A woman's body is found missing . . ."

"When her sister goes missing, the other sister lends a hand . . ."

"When her sister's hands go missing . . ."

"When the female detective—who is unlucky in love and is, by the way, sexy, and searching for a missing girl—without hands goes missing . . ."

Most fiction thrillers are about a woman dying. Something about women dying is more beautifully tragic. It gets your atten-tion more than "When Jeff from Home Depot dies in his car . . ."

Meanwhile, thrillers for men usually start with:

"When a briefcase is stolen . . ."

"The president calls on an old friend to serve justice . . ."

"An ex-con with a heart of gold and a drinking problem has to save the world at sixty."

"Despite swearing to an oath of peace, Trent McFist leaves the orphanage he's dedicated his life to to steal back a rare diamond, which can save the world and also sort of avenge his wife's death. He has to prove to himself that he can do this one last mission and that he's still really good at hand-to-hand combat . . . at ninety-five."

So what is the rule? Death is glamorous and fascinating if it's a woman dying, but not if it involves a baby, because babies are innocent and all women . . . have it coming? Or is it deeper? A sexualized woman ripped away from life is gorgeously tragic, but a baby isn't sexy (legally), so it's just tragic?

We need to talk about miscarriages more in a public-health-conversation way, if only to intellectually prepare you for a possible outcome. Then again, who would want to listen to a story about a miscarriage if they hadn't had one?

> And if they had had one, who would want to hear about someone else's? The topic of periods is a great example. I'm disgusted at how precious our society is about something that happens to around half of our population, AND YET if I'm reading a book and the author starts talking about the weirdness that is getting a first period, I skip ahead. Not because it's gross but because it's boring to me. Every time I get mine, it's not a big deal. I even rolled my eyes while typing these last few sentences.

I want new information. So here is what I'll say about miscarriages that most people sort of already know. According to the Mayo

Clinic, 10–20 percent of all known pregnancies end in miscarriages. And no one is talking about it! To put it in perspective, only about 5 percent of men forty and under have erectile dysfunction, but we ALL know about Viagra and how easy it is to obtain a prescription, that the pill is blue, and that "if the erection lasts more than four hours to call a doctor . . . or a party planner." We know this because of the commercials. Male "health" issues are widely discussed. What do you do if you have a miscarriage? Do you go to the emergency room? Do you just walk it off? What if you have a miscarriage but your body doesn't tell you it happened? Well, that happened to me.

I want to share my story really because I don't think there is anything to be ashamed of or embarrassed about. If women's health were less of a taboo issue, we would all be a lot healthier and happier. Maybe there should be a *Law & Order* about miscarriages? *L&O: D&C* (Note: Read this in the narrator's voice from the opening of the show).

"In the reproductive health-care system, the attention given to women's bodies is especially heinous. In the US, the women affected by reproductive issues that almost no one cares about are often shamed out of sharing what happened to them. These are their stories [my story]. KA-CHUNG . . ."

I was quietly pregnant ("quietly" meaning I hadn't told the Internet. I had told every woman in my life despite my husband suggesting I wait.). "Okay, but just Vanessa because she's secretly pregnant too! Which I only found out after I told her I was secretly pregnany."

On a keyboard, the T and the Y key are right next to each other, and, since I was always texting *super* fast about how excited I was to be pregnant, I was often accidentally typing "pregnany," and to this day my best friend and I both say "pregnany" instead of "pregnant."

I went in for my six-week checkup, and I heard a heartbeat. Wow. Teeny thing. *Whoosh, whoosh.* So fast. Working so hard. There it was. It was too early to tell the sex, so we called the baby Mango. I don't know why, other than it was a fun word to say and the little fetus's bean shape reminded me of a mango. I also love mangos. We didn't want to give it a *kenahora*, a Yiddish word my mom uses, which basically means you don't want to jinx it by naming a baby at such an early stage.

Did you know that in Jewish tradition it's not only bad luck to name a baby before it's born, but to buy anything for it? Movies always show expecting moms, fully pregnany, painting a nursery, inhaling paint fumes. What they don't show is the parents using that nursery as an office because she ends up miscarrying.

But I told everyone in my family.

I am a terrible secret keeper. I love sharing things, and I will always tell at least one person a secret you told me unless you make a really big deal about it, then I'll probably only tell a few people who you don't know.

I went in for our ten-week checkup. From the second I walked in, it was a bad vibe.

I had left my ob-gyn for greener pastures (aka she went out of network and I was like "I love you but not enough to pay for you!"), and this was my first time seeing this new doctor.

I walked into the office, which seemed to be under construction. Exposed beams, unpainted drywall, no décor—it was like the office in *Boiler Room*. No matter. I'm a Millennial; we're the generation that sought out hidden-gem noodle places in strip malls—I don't let facades dissuade me.

The nurses didn't make eye contact or say much other than, "Fill this out and give a urine sample. First date of your last period?" A little cold, but okay. Also, I don't know that answer. I know I should keep track of these things, and I always mean to, but I forget. I did some math. "August second, I think?"

I peed and then, not seeing a designated area for my cup of warm urine, I poked my head out from the bathroom door. "Should I leave this here on the toilet, or name it and carry it around with me?" "Just put it over there," she said. Without gesturing in any particular direction. "Just there, where? In the ether?" I thought, *Should I atomize this urine or just burn it like sage?* "Over there," she said again, gesturing to *literally* nothing.

> There is this weird tension that arises when you ask an already annoyed and overworked office person to be specific about something they believe they were clear about. In her mind, "over there" is where all the pee goes forever because she references it a thousand times a day and regular patients know. To me, it could have been anywhere from in the toilet bowl to on the floor to one of the four exam rooms that were open. Also, I was holding my hot pee in a cup, so I felt, like, weirdly vulnerable.

A nurse popped out of one of the rooms and waved me in. I came in and took the liberty of setting my pee down. She took my blood pressure. Said nothing to me. She didn't tell me to uncross my legs, didn't tell me to stop holding my phone IN THE ARM that was wrapped in the blood pressure sleeve. No talking. No anything. Fine. I was just there to see the doctor, whatever. And I'm sure she sees a thousand pee-toting people a day, so we didn't have to be best friends. Another nurse came in for some more info. "First date of your last period?" Of course my thought was, *Wasn't this written down just five minutes ago?* I told her August 2. She wrote it down. "Eleeza Scelsinger." It's Iliza. Shlesinger. "Kay," she said and walked out. I took the "kay" as a concession to the phonetics instead of an agreement that I actually knew my own name.

> What always floors me is 99 percent of people's inability to pronounce Iliza or SHHHH-LESS-SINGER. Schwarzenegger everyone can say. I get that his name is said *a lot* more, but still. Even crazier to me is that no one can say or spell Iliza (LLIZA, LIZA, ELIZA, IIZARD) and for sure no one can spell Shlesinger, but when they try, people always put a C in there. Total morons will write "ELSA SCHELSIGNER." And what I'm always amazed by is their lack of basic comprehension skills but their firm grasp on German phonetics. Because they're right: There *should* be a C in Shlesinger. I'm told my great grandfather took it out at Ellis Island to make it sound "less Jewish"—great job.

This nurse had on the standard nurses' scrubs, a standard mask, a standard stethoscope, standard nurse sneakers, and a gold necklace with a charm of an AK-47. What.

I'm not a medical professional, but . . . not standard? I'm pretty sure those aren't hospital-issued. I don't think FIGS makes those necklaces.

We live in a society where women, specifically white women, have come under fire for "acting entitled." They get called any range of diminutive things from "spoiled" to "Karen." In many cases, I think that's fair: You aren't special just because you feel entitled, regardless of color or gender. What isn't right is how we now malign almost any woman who speaks up about anything that might make them uncomfortable. Any woman who doesn't go with the flow. We've gotten to this weird place where, somehow, any white woman over thirty is a monster, but we don't take the same aim at white men. Notice that there are no Kevins, only Karens. I get that everything can't be my way all the time, but weirdly, I draw the line at symbols of death in the workplace. Call me old-fashioned.

You're a nurse. Nurses are like tough angels! You aid people in living, basically. There is no alternative use for an AK-47. You could even wear a swastika and argue it was originally used in Sanskrit to mean "well-being" (you'd be an asshole, but you wouldn't be incorrect). Guns are used for killing. An AK-47 isn't even used for hunting. It is one of the more offensive, tone-deaf things a nurse can wear. And I was horrified that this necklace was what I had to stare at during this already terrible visit to a gynecologist.

I said nothing because chances are if you find that necklace acceptable to wear to work you won't change your mind because I challenged you on it.

Then the doctor came in. I said to her, "Ya know . . . I'm really nervous being here because I've never been pregnant before and the vibe here is a little weird." When I had looked her up, the reviews were, "Doc is great; staff is horrible," so I assumed this wasn't earth-shattering news to her. And I was watering this feedback down as much as possible. Patients should have a right to say how they are feeling, and I shouldn't have to feel nervous and grateful to be at a doctor's office. She was practical and overworked, and simply said, "Well, it's Covid." "Well, it's Covid" is the social equivalent to "There is literally nothing anyone can or will do. And you're already here, so . . ."

The exam began. Awkward. Like, have you ever filled out a comment card while someone is partially inside you?

The next thing she said to me was, "I'm not hearing a heartbeat."

Instantly humbled by the fact that I had been focused on office demeanor when my baby was dead, I held my breath. Maybe she couldn't hear the heartbeat over the deafening shine of the nurse's exquisite AK-47 GOLD CHARM BLING-BLINGING IN THE LIGHT!

Now I'm lying on my back, surrounded by strangers, with my legs open . . . crying into my mask during a vaginal ultrasound. The doctor softened. Clearly, this wasn't an anomaly to her, and it probably wasn't the only time it had happened that week or maybe even that day. She showed me that the baby wasn't measuring very big; it seemed as if it had stopped growing soon after I had heard the tiny heartbeat a few weeks ago. *Whoosh, whoosh.*

She said there was an expert she wanted to refer me to, just in case the heartbeat was so faint she couldn't hear it. I saw a sliver of hope, and I clung to it. She said he wasn't far, that I could even walk.

So I did. It was a block, but it's LA, so it felt like a lot farther. Also, I was crying. Also, the vaginal ultrasound jelly was just now finding its way out of my body. I was sweating, crying, and glooooooping.

I arrived at the new doctor, sweaty, sad, and gloopy.

In my life I've never *ached* for kids the way many women do, or the way we are told we are supposed to. I've never felt the universe was rubbing another woman's family in my face until that moment on that day. The office had four couples waiting, all with children. And yeah, I judged them! The dads were all ugly. There, I said it.

So I'm crying in my mask, squishy, in a waiting room while being forced to listen to children whining to their ugly dads. I just kept to myself, balled up in the corner, desperately wanting the nurse to call my name.

"Eleeza? Selsinger?" That's me! I am ELEEZA SELSINGER!

I got up and walked with the nurse. "First date of your last period?"

Is there some sort of, I don't know, network of the future where offices can trade information on patients via some sort of inter-net-like system? Or is it like they're quizzing you to make sure you're the same patient you said you were?

The nurse was very sweet, and the doctor was nice—why wouldn't they be?

I lay down. I had never had a man (who I wasn't kissing) look at my vagina before. So I kissed my doctor right on the mouth. Kidding, but, ya know, it's my preference to have a female ob-gyn, and as I walked in and saw my doctor was a man, I just thought, *No, this is perfect.*

I love a self-inflicted emotional pile-on. Maybe it's the comic in me (the darkness), but a story isn't funny if only one thing goes wrong. You having a bad day has to be several hours of bullshit for the story to be fun for someone to hear when you retell it, laughing, later. Like an itemized receipt you present to the universe at the end where you show each injury and each insult added up to total a catastrophe. And I believe the universe gives you a karmic rebate after that, even if it only comes in the form of late-night frozen yogurt, a mud mask, and a movie . . . and cheese. But it was perfect that the day was so shitty and to top it off I had to see a male gynecologist.

Dr. No Kisses confirmed there was, in fact, no heartbeat. I looked over at the sonogram monitor. Why? Why would I do that? Is it a weird artistic urge to torture myself? And what was I expecting I'd see on that screen, the credits running? I think I thought it would be horrific, but it was, visually, and this is the only way I can describe it: quiet. There was my tiny Mango, a little bean lying on its side. My only thought was that it looked so lonely in the dark. A womb is supposed to be a warm (bloody) place filled with life, and that day it looked like Mango had fallen to the bottom of a dark well, only a light from the ultrasound wand illuminating it from the top. I felt so bad for her (I wanted Mango to be a girl). She was all alone. I know she wasn't a full baby—it was so early, she was just a collection of cells—but still.

Now is when you get to think, *But you said in your last book,* Girl Logic, *that you had an abortion—don't you think that baby was all alone?* And to that I say this: If your friend died, you would cry, but if you heard a stranger died, you probably wouldn't. The difference is love. And I wanted this one to be alive, and I tried very hard to make it happen. A woman should be the one to decide to try very hard to make it happen and to keep a baby; the government shouldn't decide for her.

But here was my problem.

Baby was dead + Baby hadn't left my body = Baby was still in me but not alive.

So what was happening?

I had had a "missed" miscarriage, Dr. No Kisses told me. Which meant my body never, like, *got the memo* that the pregnancy wasn't viable (I'm trying to find alternative phrases to "dead baby" because it's enough already, but I'm not a fan of the word "fetus," so just bear with me.). I don't know if it was that my body didn't *get* the memo or never *sent* the memo, but, the point is, I still had the baby in me. Dead.

I know this is not right, but I felt like an idiot. Being so careful, eating well, reading all the ingredients on my bath and body products, buying all the books, okay, I was *gifted* one book and only read a quarter), getting excited, talking to my belly for weeks . . . and it wasn't alive. I know I'm being hard on myself, but I am also sure that in sharing that sentiment, someone else out there will feel a little less horrible, so it's fine. I'm fine. You're fine too. You will be fine.

Then I turned on myself, as I frequently do when I'm mad. I was mad at my body; it had lied to me! "WHEN WERE YOU GONNA TELL ME?!" How long was my body gonna keep that secret?! "You embarrassed us! How long were you gonna let us walk around saying we were pregnant? I TOLD A CASHIER AT A HOMEWARES STORE IN SAN DIEGO THAT I WAS PREGNANT! We had a moment! She let me use the employee bathroom! And then my husband read this book and found out I had told another person I was pregnant! Ahh! Oops! I can't keep a secret!

> If you think about it, your body can't be trusted. You wash it, you stretch it, you nourish it, and yeah, it might take you

places, but it harbors deep genetic secrets. Your DNA knows what's gonna happen, and it doesn't tell you! It laughs at you! "Guess what! I had a cancer gene this whole time! Enjoy our hair now because there will be none in five years! Enjoy this waist now, for soon I WILL BE THICKER! Oh, what's that? A crick in your neck? Nope! It's herniated discs; I've been leaking spinal jelly THIS WHOLE TIME. Also I have gas and I'm not gonna release it to your butthole *just* so you think the mounting pressure in your body is a heart attack! Wake up! It's me! Your foot! I'm throbbing in the middle of the night, but it's such a weirdly specific throb you don't know how to describe it and by morning I'll be gone! Gone but not forgotten! Maybe I'll be back. I hope you're worried! Hope you don't look too tired! Oh, by the way! You are always going to look tired! And that will stress you out! So much that it will manifest itself as . . . You know that lump? It's nothing. JK! It's something! Maybe! I'll never tell until ya cut me open!"

So the hope of passing it naturally was a dashed one. The doctor casually said, "we can just do a D&C." Now, many of you know this term. Clinically, it means "dilation and curettage." I, however, had never heard of it because, again, all things female-health-related live in a locked box in a shame cabinet in the back closet of our health-care system under a Bible filled with cash. But D&C is a colloquialism for "dusting and cleaning." The casual nature of an abbreviated name belies the invasiveness. Basically? To be hard-core about it? They just go in and suck the mass out of your womb. It's basically an abortion procedure. And you, as a woman, are supposed to be very cool and private about this. V casual. No biggie. Be cool. Stay cool. Have a great summer. H.A.G.S.

It was a Wednesday. You only need to know that info because of what happened next. The doctor said, "We can do the D&C next Thursday." *NEXT* THURSDAY?! Not *tomorrow* Thursday—*next* week's Thursday.

> Translation: "Can you carry around your dead fetus even longer? You've already carried it around for several weeks, what's another eight days? You're a woman, it's fine. Be cool! Don't complain! Smile!"

Physically, I'm sure it would have been easy. But mentally, that was one of the most brutal things I ever heard. It felt like one of the options in *Saw*.

> I should tell you that with all the variations of sadness I was experiencing, not once did it occur to me that I should feel any emotion toward the idea that I now had to tell everyone I had lost this baby. I wasn't nervous to do it, I wasn't scared, I wasn't anything. This was my story, this was my experience, and I don't keep people in my life who don't understand me.

Meanwhile, I pay dues to two entertainment unions. I have two insurances. I live in a major city, and I was going to a great hospital. And I am of a certain tax bracket. I am saying these things because, historically, these facts have amounted to receiving "good" treatment. Even with all these things, I was still told to hold on to my dead baby for eight days . . . I can't imagine the health care a woman with darker skin or lower economic standing receives. Women's health care isn't personal, it's political. It's social, and it affects all of us. Every community. We are all connected. We have to take better care of women so our communities can be healthier.

And yes, I already believed that, and it took me having a miscarriage to know that on a personal level. Sometimes, unfortunately, we have to experience things to truly be in a place to fight for them. This is why I'm so vocal about women's health both onstage and off, on social media and in real life. You know what no one wants to talk about, drunk, at a bar? Reproductive rights. You know what one of my favorite topics and pastimes is? I'm a fun hang!

I called my friend and physician (I think she was my physician who became my friend. Years ago, she let me bring my [since passed] dog Blanche into her office for a photo shoot [A DOG WITH A STETHOSCOPE! PRINT IT ON A CARD!]). She was no longer my doctor, but I told her the story. She was *horrified* because this had all happened at her hospital group. She made a call for me. She got me in with a great doctor for the next day. It shouldn't have required me knowing someone, but, like most accessible privilege in life, it did. I walked into my new doctor's office. I was so tired from being sad, and I was so afraid of another AK-47 *Boiler Room* office situation—but this office was nice. There were chairs! She came in and talked with me, and I, through my glassy eyes, like an orphan kitten looking up at a golden retriever for maternal guidance, said, "Will you be my new doctor?" And she said yes.

You're wondering where my husband was through all of this? He was outside, waiting. Covid has robbed so many parents of shared doctors' visits and support.

I was given two options. Take a pill that forces your body to pass the tiny Mango at home. Or door number two: Come in for a D&C

the next day. Having not experienced any of this, I thought it was better to have this done with a doctor versus at home with no medical supervision, frontier-style. I was warned there would be blood. Blood on its own doesn't bother me, but blood is a lot scarier when it's coming out of you and you don't know how much there should be or when it will stop. She gave me a pill that softens the uterus. She said to take it the night before I came in for the D&C.

I did not know there would be contractions.

What a fucking raw deal. No baby but some of the the pain of a baby? I woke up around one A.M. to the worst, what I can only describe as period cramps, as it is my only frame of reference for the twisting pain that happens (guys, it's like having the worst gas of your life, but it's only in your testicles). I just lay there trying to breathe through it. It went on for several hours. I thought, *For all of this pain, I could have just done it at home! Could have spared myself the Covid test and drive across town!*

I lay on the bed, one hand on my belly and one hand on the dog, secretly hoping her ancient animal healing powers would soothe me. They didn't, and she moved away to lick herself.

Finally, it was seven A.M.—time to go to the doctor's office.

I went in, I lay down, and they gave me twilight anesthesia.

Twilight anesthesia is so fun, oh my God. Like, a miscarriage is horrible, for sure, but that drug was great. So you're awake but feel nothing, and when it's done you remember nothing. Pro tip? Don't have your phone in your hands if you get twilight anesthesia. Don't have your phone if you have any medically admitted narcotic. Because a few weeks later your friend Marcie will text you to say she has Covid and you will be so mad because you saw her the week before and what if she exposed you and then she will say, "The second I tested positive, you were the first person I told" and then you look up the date and realize you had been texting with her through your anesthesia the whole time. You also ordered two hundred dollars' worth of Indian food (so, like, three things) on Grubhub. To an old address. You also texted your agent that you think "we should go for it and make *Central Intelligence*," the Kevin Hart movie from 2016.

Going in, I was positive I would remember it.

I've always been a very coherent drinker, and I can't say I've ever "blacked out" as much as I just went to sleep, really hard. I tend to have very long and deep conversations when I'm bombed. People rarely know I'm drunk, and I take myself very seriously. My best friend said, "Your MO when you're high is to swear you are sober." Like, if there is a life-changing conversation to be had while trashed in a women's bathroom about self-esteem or a shitty boyfriend? I will HAVE that conversation with you! We were out with a group of friends at a bar in Nashville one time, and my husband noticed that a guy had been talking to me for a while, so he came over to check on me (really to make sure the guy wasn't scaring me), and he heard this snippet: "feminism can't be treated as a unilateral issue," and he was like, "Oh, she's fine." Also, with a sentence like that, we are *positive* the guy didn't think I was flirting.

I don't remember what I said to the nurses, but I'm sure I talked the whole time. I love talking to people. Gotta be weird for the nurses to talk to patients and answer their questions knowing the answer doesn't matter because the patient is awake-sleep talking.

I remember coming to. The drugs wear off so fast, unfortunately. Such a shame because it's so rare to have a professionally induced, medically controlled, SAFE high . . . Can't we keep this party going just a *moment* longer? Maybe a sidecar for the ride home? I remember asking if I could just have a little more and thinking the doctor would *for sure* say yes. I was like, "You seem cool—you'll do it, right?" She definitely would not do it. And then I remember saying to her, "Do you want to see a picture of my dog?" And she said, laughing, "You already showed us, hon."

So a miscarriage is a big deal. It's an even bigger deal the later in a *pregnany* you have one. But it's not something from which I am still reeling. And while I am resilient, I think talking about this experience onstage, sharing this with other women and them sharing their emotions back, is what made processing it easier. It wasn't until I had a miscarriage that I realized how many women had had them and how ready so many women, and couples in general, were to open up about theirs. Women are incredible creatures with so much kindness and a wealth of compassion and sympathy born of empathy. But we are so used to being treated like absolute shit, maligned, and pitted against one another, I think it's easy to forget that we actually have more in common with one another than society wants us to realize.

But, looking back, the physical act of the miscarriage itself truly isn't a big deal. It's the end of a pregnancy, for sure, and that part is a big deal, but the actual procedure takes mere moments, doesn't hurt, and the scariest part, as with most things, is the anticipation. If we're being honest? Being put totally under for the epidural for my herniated discs was a lot scarier. I just went back and reread those last two sentences . . . Who am I? I'm supposed to be twenty-five, on the road, doing stand-up and getting drunk at a club. When did I get this old?

While it would have been better to just, ya know, have a baby, this experience brought a new depth to my perspective on being a woman. And I think, as an artist, making horrible experiences relatable to an audience is a rewarding part of my job.

But I toggle between PEOPLE NEED TO KNOW EVERYTHING ABOUT MY BABY JOURNEY and no one needs to know anything.

I tend to share things because I think, while dark, they can still be funny, like the above story. I also don't believe I have anything to be ashamed of, and I don't think any woman has anything to be ashamed of when it comes to her body. And it's why I'm gonna share this next, equally exhausting, story.

That whole story happened in September 2020. By January of 2021, I still wasn't pregnant—no more mangos. My doctor said I was perfectly fine. "Just relax," she said. I thought, *Yeah right, have you seen my act?* But something told me to see a specialist (that "something" was my mother-in-law and my mother, and my stepmother-in-law, and my father-in-law), just in case. I felt like my fertility hubris was wounded at the hint of the idea that conception might not be as easy as it was promised (or, depending on your age, threatened). Here is my one piece of concrete advice I will pass on to any woman who has unsuccessfully tried to get pregnant:

GO SEE A FERTILITY SPECIALIST.

Of course, sadly, not everyone is able to do this. But in a perfect world (where I'm, like, *a little taller*, with natural highlights framing my face) where we have a functioning health-care system that doesn't leave women in a lower income bracket in the dust and where obstetrics gets as much attention as the advancement in boner medicine does, we would be proactive about women's fertility issues so as not to cause further problems, not just keep telling them to "try harder and relax harder."

I'm also incredibly torn on discussing how I was able to get pregnant. Because even discussing attempting to get pregnant invites everyone to tell you how they did it, what worked for their body, and it becomes less of a conversation and more of a declaration. A relative ten years older than me who doesn't have a partner said, "Do IUI; don't even wait." And another female friend, who is married to a woman, said, "Just go right to IVF."

Because those were things that worked for *them*. No one considered I was thirty-eight, healthy, had gotten pregnant before, and had a husband with tested, normal sperm and a working penis. In the end, we did it the old-fashioned way. By doing a few progesterone shots and having perfectly timed sex! INSTANT BABY!

There is no lonelier feeling than having to give yourself a hormone shot. Noah would do it normally, but when I had to go on the road for a few days, it was just me, a THICK-ASS twenty-one-gauge needle, progesterone oil, and an alcohol swab. I had to pump myself up with locker-room hype the first few times, like, *You've come this far! You gonna let a little needle stand in the way of you and a baby? It's go time! Do it! Champions do more! So many women have to do so much more; it's just a shot! Do it! Three-two-one, GO TEAM!* After a few times, it got easier. One time I got a little too cocky and I'm pretty sure I hit a bone; nothing more humbling than crying with your pants down alone in a theater bathroom minutes before you have to do an hour of stand-up.

But I'm not ashamed of my journey. I don't need to fool people into thinking I'm flawlessly fertile; Am I a horse for auction? Who cares?

In fact, I think this mandate that all women be ever-fertile and we rarely consider the man's fertility is archaic. Ladies, please listen to me. You having trouble having a baby has nothing to do with your value or your womanhood. All right? I think we need to keep saying it until we all actually believe it. I can say it to you, but I can't lie, I definitely felt bad about myself when it wasn't as easy as I had hoped. I didn't feel worthless, God, no. I just was a little bummed it didn't come easier.

But there is a weird unspoken shame when it comes to fertility.

> I have a relative who, when I told her I did progesterone shots, somehow got it in her mind that we did IVF. We didn't. And we had at least two conversations where she said, "So, now, I know you did IVF, how was that?" and I found myself irritated with her. Because, if I really think about it, it felt like she was categorizing *all* fertility treatment as IVF. I wondered if she was inadvertently doing this because we like to think other women had it as hard as we did, which, in a way, makes us feel less bad about our own struggle. Even more reason for the conversations around fertility to be less cloaked. There is nothing to feel bad about!

I had had no medical issues my whole life and I could get pregnant, so I thought, *Why would I need to see a specialist?* Right? Because when you think "fertility specialist," you think IVF or IUI, or you think women leaving offices in tears; stuck with hormones; bogged down by expensive bills; embryo adoption; sterile, regimented sex. But it isn't that. There can be a painfully simple reason it isn't happening for you, and it can have nothing to do with any of that.

It can be something as simple as a polyp that caused your miscarriage.

You could be having all the sex in the world and getting all the acupuncture and taking all the herbs and supplements and doing all the morning hobbit yoga, doing all the de-stressing . . . but you could have a polyp. And a polyp is a polyp is a polyp. You can't relax it away.

There's a weird layer of shame around an inability to get pregnant on command. Since the dawn of time, "barren women" have been outcasts, and lack of fertility made you a less desirable mate, etc.

> You know what I think about all the time? How often, histori-
> cally, women were just deemed "barren." In actuality, they prob-
> ably had polyps or, like, the simplest medical issue that the
> science of the time couldn't handle. Or it was the guy. It was
> some super-old king and his sad, weird sleepy sperm. I also
> think about the array of mental disorders that affect people
> and how most of those went undiagnosed for the majority of
> our time on earth as humans. 100 percent chance that most
> maniacal kings were bipolar or fully schizophrenic. Or serial
> killers in ermine robes.

So who would want to go to a specialist? Who would want to admit they aren't as juicy and fertile as they are supposed to be? Isn't that what we require of women? That they be young and flexible and smooth and plump and fun and horny and innocent and thin but meaty in the right places forever?

So I went. To see if anything was wrong, they had to do a procedure where they flush your uterus with water (it's fucking brutal, but you get a niblet of Valium. I'm not a drug addict, I just think it's better to focus on the pleasurable parts of medical procedures) and there it was . . . a polyp. I had a polyp. A polyp that no one would have ever found had I not opted to see a specialist. Fun fact? An ob-gyn is not a specialist and, despite the fact that something insane like three out of ten women over thirty get polyps, THEY AREN'T SOMETHING YOUR DOCTOR CHECKS FOR. Please read that again. At your regular gynecological visit, that doctor does not screen for polyps. So if you don't see a specialist and something isn't visibly wrong based on the limited checkup they do, they will tell you everything is fine. And everything *was* fine, except for the polyp.

So there I was, with no symptoms. No bleeding. No pain. Just *wasting* good sex trying to have a baby, being told I was fine, and all the while there was a polyp possibly preventing it.

The first available procedure to have it removed was February 22, which is also my birthday. So, of course, I had to steer into that skid. What's sadder than having surgery *ON* your uterus *ON* your birthday? Hilarious.

It gets worse, but only to people who live in Los Angeles.

> It couldn't be at the local hospital in Hollywood; the procedure is only done at a hospital in Redondo Beach, forty-five min from my house. In LA, "forty-five minutes away" is basically you kissing your loved ones good-bye forever. Perhaps you'll write to them.
>
> The best-worst part? The surgery had to be in the afternoon to maximize my chances of afternoon traffic.

It was too horrible to pass up.

> I went, expecting to come home with a list of delicious reasons why that day had been the worst. But it wasn't. The check-in

nurse actually got me in a little early, and one of the nurses, having seen it was my birthday on my chart (see! People do read the info on charts, it turns out!) brought me a birthday balloon. The smallest act from the most random stranger made my day. Then I fell asleep and woke up polyp-free. Also, I woke up *super* high, and that was the greatest birthday present of all. Noah picked me up and gave me a Yuzu soda (because, of course, he killed time while I was in surgery by going to a Japanese grocery store, he's so cute) and then he drove me home while I rambled. And then I got to eat sushi for my birthday dinner and have some drinks! Yes, please.

But after all of that, it wasn't a polyp.

It was *three* fucking polyps! And the doctor said, "I can say with confidence that this is what caused your miscarriage," and I kicked myself that I didn't go see her sooner. I only wasted four months, but still, that's like half a baby.

A BABY! TELL ME EVERYTHING

I actually don't know why any woman publicly states anything about how she raises her child. It's a one-way ticket to personal scrutiny from the masses. It's a great way to feel deeply and personally attacked about the thing most important to you by people who have no stock in you. It's just another thing that causes anxiety, rifts, secret judgment, and forced and unnecessary competition between women.

Even toward the end of my pregnancy in the last few days of waiting, posting anything about it, nothing that suggested I didn't know what I was doing, but a mere status update, brought on hundreds of comments from strangers about what I should be doing. "Have sex to bring on labor!" "Stimulate your nipples!" "Have more sex, girl!" "Work those nips!"

It's incredibly disconcerting to have strangers yell at you to play with your own nipples. A woman is commanded, her whole life, to have sex with no one and then, because she's pregnant, somehow it's okay to scream at her "GET TO FUCKIN'!" People just hurling that advice unsolicited is one of the weirdest things I experienced during my pregnancy.

Despite all of this, I do believe there is a bond created by sharing with people who actually want to connect with you. To confide anything about your choices as a mother, prenatally or postpartum, is to enter into a binding agreement that you are sharing this information from a vulnerable place. And if you are listening to this information, you should be taking it in, as my aunt Debbie says, "from the highest light" (meaning you are giving input only from the best place, wanting the best for that person and having nothing to do with shaming, insecurities, or a personal agenda).

An example of the highest light would be if you told a friend:

"We haven't even looked into preschool yet, I think we are gonna keep him home for a bit." And your friend says, "Every child learns differently, so whatever works for you. But if you end up wanting a preschool, I have a great recommendation." What is not from the highest light and is, in fact, from a dark place of insecurity and resentment is someone responding, "Oh, you are already behind; if they aren't in the right preschool they basically don't have a path to any college. Is your child good at picking up garbage? Because that's what their life will be. We've already put our son into three preschools; good luck slumming it at a federally run day care, future proud mom of a walking trash can!"

I remember going to the checkup to hear my baby's heartbeat at sixteen weeks. I remember the doctor telling me, "It's a perfect heartbeat!" Which was all I cared about. The exact number was something with the number 9. Could have been 197 or 90 (I just went and looked up the ideal heartbeat for a fetus at sixteen weeks: The answer is between 110 and 160 beats per minute . . . Oops. Maybe it was 149? I can feel you reading this thinking, *What kind of a monster doesn't remember her baby's EXACT HEARTBEAT NUMBER from a billion weeks ago?! Take away her baby! Give it to the state!*

Anyway, I went for coffee (YES, IT WAS JUST THE ONE CUP) with a friend whose wife was also pregnant at the same time. We had both just had the same heartbeat appointment. Casually, he asked, "So . . . what was your baby's heartbeat?"

> I couldn't help but read into that question. I thought, *What's it to ya?* The doctor said it was perfect; are we doing a side-by-side comparison of whose baby is superior based on this number? BECAUSE THE ANSWER IS MINE. She's sixteen weeks, with no eyebrows, and she is a SUPERIOR QUEEN TO ALL OTHER UNBORN BABIES!

I just opted out of the conversation by saying, "I don't remember, but they said it was fine . . . Wanna share a muffin?" He did!

On a more invasive but less interpersonal note: A random fan asked to see my belly, my bare belly, once. Totally well-intentioned (I think), but I've never given something a harder, quicker pass in my life. Moms, don't worry about how and when you will set up personal boundaries; your brain takes over, and you do it automatically. Almost like a mama bear.

> Hm, I wonder if anyone has ever made that connection before? Someone should definitely inscribe it on a water bottle or emboss it on a tote bag . . . Maybe in glitter? What's a great way to upcharge for a canvas tote? Maybe glittered cursive *mama bear* on the front, but the other side says *but a wolf in the bedroom!* Something to let strangers know the person carrying this tote is a mother bear, but still, also, a sexual bear. Maybe

something like, on a pink wine tumbler that says *wolf juice, but then,* excuse me, wrong font . . . but then on the tote it says, *she wolf . . . she believed she could so she wolfed.* We need the right messaging; otherwise, people won't know you're a woman with a child but also have a personality, you SHE-BEAR-WOLF-DIVA! PRINT IT ON STILETTO AND MAKE IT INTO A TIARA!

No one had ever asked to see my belly before—abs, yes, which I often show off unsolicited, but pregnant belly, no. And the second they asked, I knew that wasn't something I would do. I share a lot as a public figure, but I knew going into my pregnancy that I wasn't signing up for further scrutiny if I could help it. You can criticize my art, my stand-up, my looks, but the masses don't get to be part of this pregnancy in any way I can't control. Show my belly? Maybe parts of it, but you will never get full-frontal naked belly. Yeah right, I'm not gonna show my pregnant belly so someone can screen-grab it and jerk off to it. It's not up for judgment. It can be the most perfect, shiny, taut tummy in the world, or it can be the most natural, stretch-mark-laden, purple, contorted tummy gourd, and no one but me (and Noah and some doctors and some nurses and maybe a few friends and relatives) will ever know!

Moreover, shaming women for their choices about how they raise their child is this weird God-given right people feel they have.

Is the woman feeding her baby cigarettes? Then yes, say something. Is she breastfeeding till the kid is three? Who cares. She isn't breastfeeding *your* kid. She isn't breastfeeding *you.* Plenty of people were raised according to doctor-recommended specificities, and they went on to become murderers, so let's not declare that what works for one mother works for all mothers or that there is one righteous path to parenting.

Also? Let's say the mom *does* do something you don't agree with and the kid *does* turn out weird and you *can* pinpoint it to that specific choice she made? ("He shot a cat? Ya know, I saw this coming because I remember that one day she let him watch too much TV.") Then you get the delicious retribution of saying, "I told ya so!" Privately, to another friend who agrees with you.

Most people don't feel a fierce devotion toward other people's children, but somehow when it comes to armchair judgment, they are deeply invested and total experts. A lot of society is obsessed with *forcing* women to become mothers, but why do we feel that once a woman is a mother then no woman knows what she's doing? That's because hating women is a national pastime, and judging mothers is an elevated form of that sport.

People love to hate the mother with the crying baby in first class. As if money or lack of money qualifies your parenting skills. Like a kid with an earache cares what tax bracket you're in. I fly almost every week, and I can promise you, just because you had an extra thousand dollars or built up enough random SkyMiles flying Phoenix to Chicago to get into seat 1A, doesn't make you any less of a monster or more down-to-earth than the guy sitting in 34Z with his shoes off and a sleeveless THESE COLORS DON'T RUN shirt, mask just below his nose. But yes, a comedy rule and a rule in society is that it's always more acceptable to punch up and make fun of a "rich" person than a "poor" person.

I said "mother" because you almost never see a dad, especially in first class, flying alone with a baby. If he did, I'm sure he would qualify for sainthood. The moms doing it all, flying solo with two children under five, or the pregnant woman flying with an infant—they are the ones who deserve special treatment. There's also something so weirdly despondent about a woman flying alone with children. She could be flying from her family's house in Aspen to join her husband on their yacht in Miami, but, in transit, she is a struggling single mother. I had a single mother raise me for a long time, and I can tell you, society is not kind to these women.

BUT. I get how annoying it is when you pay a lot of extra money for first class and there is a crying baby. You paid more for an experience, and that experience doesn't include a screaming baby. And what's worse is that somehow, people think that the mother *wants* this to be happening, that she isn't doing *all* she can to calm her child. I think people think that with every cry the mother whispers, "Yes! Another! With every tear, I grow younger and more powerful!" When a first-class ticket is involved, we always prioritize our own precious three hours of in-flight relaxation over everything. This mother is struggling and traveling alone with a child, but I need silence to watch these six episodes of *Friends* on the American Airlines Gogo in-flight app! Gimme dat tiny can of club soda and that lilliputian wedge of lemon! The truth is? Other people and their carry-on bags of misery are just a part of flying. Over the years, I have watched hundreds of mothers deal with their crying children on planes.

One time I was flying LAX to JFK, sitting next to a crying baby the *whole* time. Thinking I could make a difference, I asked the mom if I could hold her. I took that little fat baby and I started to make faces to distract her from whatever she was crying about . . . and she actually stopped. As a human, it's incredibly validating when a child likes you. I thought, *Oh, wow! I have the touch!* Nope. She was pooping. And then she went back to crying, even louder this time. Now I felt like it was *our* baby! And we both couldn't make her stop! And she was stinky!

Also? There is no greater rejection of your maternal vibrations than when you go to pet a strange dog and he doesn't like you. The worst is when you're single and some hot guy has some drooling Jurassic beast dog named Molly and you try to show how dateable and cool you are by bonding with Molly and she *growls* at you. It's an assault on your womanhood. It's rejection on a spiritual level because animals are supposed to love women! Women are supposed to be Mother Nature incarnate, loving beings all creatures bond with due to our ability to give life. And rather than it simply being that Molly is just not trained well by her owner, it comes off as her "sensing" you're not kind and caring, as all women are meant to be.

Anyway, I've heard my fair share of crying babies and, even when I was in my twenties and carefree, I always felt bad for the moms.

I've come up with the perfect sequel to *Snakes on a Plane*. It's *Snakes on a Plane II: Babies on a Plane Instead of Snakes*.

Oh, I CANNOT WAIT to bring my crying baby on a plane. I may even pinch her little body under her blanket to force her to cry JUST so I can bite off the head of anyone who looks at me sideways. And as I spit out their head, their head that was in mid–eye roll before I detached it from its body, I will deliver this prepared address:

"You will avert your glares and withhold judgment entirely! I am a frequent flyer! I have been on these planes for the last twenty years listening to *all* of your children cry! In fact, some of the adults on this flight are young enough that I may have even heard *you* cry at some point! Without complaint, without judgment, I endured it, through all those years! I've even tried to help! Like that woman on a DFW flight whose baby's ears hurt, and when I offered a remedy we used to use on my brother when he was little, she told me to mind my own business and went back to playing Candy Crush! I have endured your child watching *Cocomelon* SANS headphones from an iPad! I have listened to the cries of your children, and not once have I negatively remarked, sneered, or glared, and now it's your turn to hear my baby's cries! IT'S OUR TURN! IT'S OUR TIME! I'm going to sip this little plastic cup of free Cran-Apple Juice Cocktail and eat these five pretzels in a bag, and I'm going to laugh at your cries about her cries! So suffer! SUFFFFAAAHHHHH!"

I would 100 percent be air-marshaled off the plane. From the handcuffs I'd plead, "Fine, take me away, but please, let my baby stay and cry it out. We're doing the Ferber method!"

A few years ago, there was a viral video of an Olympic skier named Julia Mancuso throwing her bundled-up toddler into a snowbank. She gently tossed the smiling baby into a pile of fluffy snow outside their home. IT WAS HILARIOUS, and the kid was fine, and the world kept turning.

The bored masses of the Internet went berserk. Somehow, any woman doing anything unorthodox with her kid, anything that hasn't been voted on by the Council of Clenched Buttholes, is seen as heresy in the eyes of Child-Raising Experts (literally anyone who clicked the video). Nobody stopped to think that this woman is an Olympic skier and her world is SNOW. She knows what is powder and what is an ice sheet. She's also at her home, so she probably knows what is under that snowbank; she wasn't drop-kicking the kid down a mountain. She also wasn't *caught* doing this; she was the one who made this video and uploaded it. Don't you think that if the kid hated it or was hurt, she wouldn't have posted it to the Internet? Do we really think she would show us a video of her trying to harm her baby?

No, because we don't consider what women actually think or that they actually think.

We don't think any woman is qualified to raise a child if they merely differ from whatever is randomly acceptable in the world of motherhood on that day. Lewis Black has a joke about how no one is truly in agreement on what is healthy. He says, "Is milk good or bad?" and there isn't a resounding collective answer from the audience. Right, because there is no one perfect answer for everyone.

But the fearmongering around child-rearing doesn't only appear when you have the child. No, no, it starts much earlier.

"Are you working on having kids?"

"You'd better get on it—you don't have much time; after all, you are over nineteen, and therefore on the decline. Have you taken your womb to be appraised on *Antiques Roadshow*?"

"You should have frozen your eggs when you were ten! Who's gonna want the weird old eggs of a full-grown woman?"

"You got an education and made money before you started thinking about children? What's wrong with you? You're thirty-five? You're basically dead! Are you gonna give birth in a nursing home or just wait to do it from the grave?"

What is the benefit of the term "geriatric pregnancy"? When a man over thirty-five is trying to conceive with his wife, do we call it "geriatric ejaculation"? The doctor has your chart, and can see you aren't twenty-five; why label something that's already obvious? "Oh, I see you're bleeding red blood out of the wrinkly head brain in your head."

I know we love shaming women for aging, but I think we just love shaming people for aging. "Elder Millennial" is an accurate description of the Millennials who are older but still of that generation. I want this in print: Whoever coined the term "geriatric Millennial," you did the Devil's work with that one. The term didn't need reinventing. I CREATED THE PERFECT ZEITGEIST TERM and the world agreed because they started using it. Why stop with thirtysomethings? Why not give "senior citizens" a makeover? How about "The Decrepit" or "wilted voters" or "close-to-deaths"—just something to really drive home the point that they are old.

Then you get pregnant, and that's when all your friends who have kids start to let it all out. Because your contemporaries with kids love, *love* to warn you how horrible what you're about to embark on is, but, knowing there is no turning back, they also have to balance it with how great it is. Keep in mind, this is mostly done so that you don't walk away thinking, *Wow, Jennifer and Scott* really *hate their baby* . . .

Their reactions read like mixed reviews for a movie:

"Enjoy life while you can!"

"I might kill myself."

"Sleep? What's that?! I've been awake since March."

"Don't do it! Run! I'm kidding! Help!"

"Say goodbye to your furniture and anything nice you ever owned because once you have a baby your house will be dripping in diarrhea and vomit."

"Get ready to never see your friends!"

"I have it planned out; I'll send the kids to their grandmother's, and then I'm gonna run the car with the windows down and garage door closed."

"A terrible adventure, but so magical!"

"You will never relax again, and your head is gonna fall off, but wow, it's so worth it."

"Your happiness as you know it is over! But babies are so rewarding!"

"I ruined my life, but she really is a gift!"

"Good luck keeping that stomach tight ever again." (That one was said to me as an outro as I was walking offstage after a set by a childless male comic.)

"I hate my kids! But they're cool!"

"By the time they find my body it will be too late to resuscitate me and I'll be free."

"I only watch *Peppa Pig*, and I've forgotten how to read!"

"Children are a blessing wrapped in dirt!"

"A child's laugh pales in comparison to the blissful eternal rest awaiting me on the other side of this bullet."

And then, when you trot further down this good-intention-paved road to hell, in comes the inundation of information. The endless stream of "If you need anything, I can help."

"I have three metric tons of baby clothes; I'll have them air-dropped to you. You can pick through them like a refugee with all your spare time."

"Teach your kid to swim the day they are born; we did. Here's a spreadsheet of the most qualified hybrid dolphin-human swim instructors in your area."

"If you need any advice on classes, pediatricians, diapers, formula, or parenting the specific way I do it, just text me. Anyway, here's your check, and thanks for coming to Denny's."

My pregnancy was relatively easy, and I'm reticent to share that. Because there is a glory in misery and suffering. It makes you more relatable. Miserable people can complain; people who have it, seemingly, slightly easier cannot. People who have it harder garner immediate sympathy, and anyone who has it easier has to keep their good fortune to themselves because no one wants to hear how happy you are because it makes them feel bad about their own reality that they have total control over!

All during this pregnancy I kept thinking about how annoying and funny it would be to tell people, "So strange, I actually lost weight and got very toned these last few months. My hair got *blonder*—is that weird?" Just to watch people's faces twitch.

There's glory in honesty in stand-up; the more raw and authentic you can be, the more relatable you are, the more the audience loves you. And modern moms have found glory in the honesty of how hard being pregnant and motherhood can be. A catharsis in being brutally honest that, prior to the Internet, was reserved for hushed conversations with other mothers in a dark room. The ways in which this honesty is cathartic for the mother are threefold.

One: The woman venting gets to feel heard, and the parents listening and relating to her get to feel seen.

Two: A mother gets the sweet satisfaction of people not fully getting it. Anyone who doesn't have a kid probably doesn't believe them and just has a laugh while thinking, *There's no way it's that hard. Silly woman! No one gets thrown up on, shit on,* and *cried on at the same time!* But the mom gets to silently snicker from atop a tiny high horse (a pony?), all the while knowing that one day the naysayer will get what's coming to them.

Three: I get to tell everyone to watch out! Because I'm filled with farts! And I can't control them!

Oh my God, I didn't know about the farting! I thought it was only the *super-pregnant* women who couldn't control their farts, not me at thirteen weeks pregnant! By the way? *No one* can control their farts. A fart has to come out; your body can't stop it or reabsorb it. You can control *how* it comes out, burying it deep in your chair, hoping your pants will filter out the worst of it. But you have no control over strength and stench. And they get so stinky when you are pregnant; I don't care how pretty you are. At about thirteen weeks, I was at an outdoor comedy show. The comedy show was in a tent set up in a parking lot with picnic tables for the audience (American ingenuity in the face of Covid!). And I was just quietly farting, figuring I was getting away with it, assuming the farts were being carried downwind because no one around me was dying. My friend Jodi was sitting in front of me, and she turned around and went, "Oh my GOD!" I froze. She had sniffed me out! Then she said, "That girl in the ugly yellow dress in front of us"—it was really ugly; a velvet mustard halter dress—"won't stop farting!" I was at a crossroads. Could I allow this woman in a truly ugly dress to be blamed for my farts? If I did, it was a victimless crime, really, in that I didn't know the victim. But I felt bad—her dress was already so ugly, she had endured enough. I was also shocked at how my farts were somehow traveling upwind? I admitted it to Jodi, who of course laughed and understood. But I removed myself from the seating area to stand alone in the parking lot and just keep farting. I found myself avoiding being around other comics because I didn't want to fart on them! I looked so antisocial! If you were at that show, just know that I wasn't too cool for everyone! I was just in my own personal fart-filled Hurt Locker!

You guys . . . I have a gross-out confession, and there is no way the person I did this to is reading this book. I have a business acquaintance who is very cool and very handsome and about ten years younger than me. He wanted to catch up and come to one of my sets and offered to pick me up on the way. At the time, I was still secretly pregnant, wearing cargo pants, an XL thick black T-shirt, and an anorak to cover my lumpy body. I did my makeup really well, but I felt so blah anyway. He arrived at my door, fragrant with Tom Ford Black Bottle. He smelled like luxury, like someone who physically never had to poop and who didn't date women who pooped, like the kind of guy you would be afraid to eat in front of on a date, the kind of guy who would silently listen to you ramble all night, ask you if you wanted cocaine he kept in a diamond, and then fuck you in a bathroom and still text you the next day. He smelled great! I kissed Noah good-bye, and he, getting a look at my ride, quietly said to me, "He looks like he has Covid." I was like, "Oh, totally. Be back in an hour!" I stepped outside and saw his car, a matte gunmetal Mercedes AMG-GT—it looked like the Batmobile. I'm not a car person. I could absolutely afford that car but choose my '09 Civic all day every day. I've never cared what car a man drove, but I saw his gorgeous car and I actually giggled, my voice scaling up like an impressed teenager. "Oh my Gahhhd, is that your car?! It looks like a sleek metal gorilla!"

We got in. I'm pretty sure the seats were made of something soft and expensive like bunny belly. We cruised down the freeway. I secretly pretended I was twenty-five and we were on a date! I thought, *I'm gonna roll up to this show in this stealth bomber with this hot younger guy, and I'm not gonna explain myself to anyone! Very cool of me!*

We had a lovely chat about work and upcoming projects . . . and I was farting the whole time. Burying each one deeper than the previous one, deeper into his organic chinchilla-scrotum seats. I prayed, *Please don't let him know what's happening. It's a coupe; the fart has nowhere to go but all around us! Please don't let me get up and leave behind an indelible fart imprint in the seat! Please don't burn a hole through this leather!* I never even smelled them, so who knows where those farts even went? I remember seeing he was low on gas; maybe the farts were what was powering that car? But he never caught on. He never knew. Until now. Because I am going to gift him this book. DAVE, I FARTED IN YOUR CAR!

There has been a pendulum shift these last, I'd say ten years, in how women portray motherhood. Women now, more than ever, have the platform to be funny or simply just honest about the trials and tribulations of having children. Books, stand-up, Tik-Tok, podcasts, and Instagram—there are whole worlds filled with women getting very real not only about pregnancy woes and the realities of childbirth, but about the tornado of a life you are sucked into when you actually have the child. It's like the mom Olympics of unearthing how hard being a mother actually is. Whether it's a funny TikTok of an exhausted, zombie-gazed mom pouring a whole box of Lucky Charms into her kid's lunch box or a father relenting and just finally giving his kid an iPad so he can finally take a shit in peace.

This is a major pendulum swing from how it had been forever, where women just had kids and never talked about ripped vaginas, diapers, guts falling out, weird nipple issues, or depression. It was something only your midwife and mother discussed with you.

Even in the mid-twentieth century, childbirth was this thing a woman went to do, in pearls, while the dad had a drink and a cigar with his friends and the male doctor would smoke a cigarette in the delivery room. The mother emerged smiling, fully made-up, vagina seemingly perfect and stitched up even tighter (with or without her consent), with a well-behaved infant in her arms, grateful a man had given her a purpose in life. Any crying, bleeding, vaginal issues, or struggles were dealt with alone, shamefully, behind closed doors (with Valium).

> I'll be honest. After I gave birth, I thought, *I love my baby and the additional silver lining to all of this is now I can see my vagina whenever I want . . . because it's halfway down my thigh!*

There was such a mysterious, heavy cloak over all of it that, to this day, women, myself included, get pregnant and only then discover the battery of information "no one ever told me." And the truth is, the information is out there. There's just so much information, and not all of it is applicable to every woman. A good quarter of *What to Expect When You're Expecting* is about mothers who smoke, drink, use drugs, have preexisting conditions, have a husband on military leave, have C-sections, and various scenarios that might not pertain to you. You are paying for a full book but really only need like 40 percent of it. But the acquiring of the information is daunting! The world of pregnancy and babies is so overwhelming, and I'm afraid I simply haven't taken in the majority of the information, and I predict I won't be able to take in more as I progress. When my baby was still in my body, I was already being told to research PRESCHOOLS FOUR YEARS INTO THE FUTURE? OR FIVE? WHEN DOES A KID START PRESCHOOL? Where do I store this information? Can't be in my brain; it's too full. If

I learn about the top preschools in the LA area, where do I put my vast knowledge of nineties R&B lyrics? If I find out what baby school on the west side has a superior finger-painting program, what am I gonna do with all my memorized quotes from *Billy Madison*? If I have to weigh the pros and cons of twelve different types of hydroponically engineered German strollers, how am I gonna remember all the plot points from *Sex and the City*?! But the truth is, why would anyone want to hear about a situation they weren't in?

> Why would a teenager want to hear about an ectopic pregnancy, hormone shots, or hemorrhoids? Why would a single twentysomething want to think about freezing her eggs when at twenty-three, she's positive she'll be young forever? When I was fully pregnant, and friends would complain about day care for their one-year-old, my eyes would go shark black and my ears would turn off. Why? Because it's hard to absorb information you aren't ready to use! I WORK! I don't have time for this! I want someone else to do the research, like in high school when we did group projects! I'll just be funny and get the credit for the work!

Learning everything about pregnancy and its various stages before you're in them is like memorizing a map to a city you may never visit. Or memorizing the outcomes of someone else's choose-your-own adventure. Information is great, but you can only plan for so much, and if you spend all day forecasting the potential outcomes of every situation, you won't have time to actually live your life.

My personal hot take? You can't/shouldn't have an opinion on this until you go through it. You are ignorant if you judge the way a woman handles pregnancy or parenthood if you haven't gone through it. That's like rolling your eyes at a soldier in boot camp wondering, *Why are they acting like it's hard? It seems easy.*

What's weird about pregnancy is that not everything that happens to your body feels right. I get that your belly and breasts get bigger, sure.

But bleeding gums?

Nasal congestion?

Skin color change?

Muscle weakness?

Am I turning into a butterfly?

Exhaustion?

Hair loss?

Am I decomposing?

Possible bone density loss?

YOUR EYESIGHT CAN GO BLURRY.

So nature is telling you you are supposed to be a discolored, blind, bleeding, gelatinous, hairless, panting, exhausted mass holed up in a dark room somewhere, but thirty seconds after you give birth, society says you need to be back to your original weight, with a supertight vagina, effortlessly caring for your child while considering all the incoming advice from others and smiling the whole time . . . and somehow keeping your baby silent on a plane. Having it all. Wearing a mom scarf!

ACT LIKE A PERSON

Do I sound old when I say, "Doesn't anyone know how to behave?" or "What is wrong with people?" Do I sound crotchety when I gasp, "Honestly, has everyone just totally lost their minds?"

Or is my exasperation one of many echoes in a chamber? Do I come from a long line of other humans who have been muttering this same sentiment—totally aghast at people's inability to behave like civilized adults at markets, in crowds, at brunch, at a political debate, drunk at IHOP, in Situation Rooms, in lines for roller coasters, on spring break, and at buffets—since humans could talk?

It's not even worth expressing frustration out loud because everyone always agrees with you, but somehow, *everyone* else is also the problem. I could exasperatedly remark, "What the fuck is *wrong* with this country?" and an unvaxxed guy clutching a rocket launcher with an alternative-facts pamphlet will agree with me. So will the woman next to me who thinks the government is evil but refuses to try to get off unemployment. So will the *trustafarian* buying fifty-dollar macadamia meditation essence in a bag who leeches off his parents and the guy who just murdered two people in the name of his religion. They would all agree with me.

Most people are good. I think. Right? We all think that, for the most part, people are kind. Taking it one step further, you could say that most people are nice people. Unfortunately, "nice" is, like, the *bare minimum* personality requirement for being a part of society. It means satisfactory, a nonissue. Because nice doesn't mean intelligent, fun, aware, capable, shrewd, sensitive, tactful, tasteful, or considerate. Nice has no color; it is the color of *blah*.

It's the most tepid endorsement. "Nice" is fine for a brief interaction. The guy handing you your coffee should be nice; your UPS driver should be nice. If you describe your mother or your lover as "nice," then you either secretly don't like them or . . . no, that's it, you secretly don't like them.

> "They're nice" is a battle cry in favor of the mediocre, the superlative of the underwhelming. Even worse is the insistence that because someone is "nice" you have to like them. There was a girl my freshman year who was a friend of a friend in our friend group. She never said much of anything, and, despite her being at plenty of events, I never got a sense of her likes, passions, opinions, or character, and yet she was always there. I would say to my friend, "Do you have to bring Ashley? She never really contributes anything; it's like bringing a sack of laundry." And my friend would always treat me like I was a monster. "Oh, stop, she's nice." The indictment on my character being that I had the audacity to be bored by a girl I had to hang out with every weekend who added nothing but was technically not doing anything "wrong." Looking back? I think everyone wanted Ashley around because she sold them Adderall.

NICE.

It's the badge everyone earns for showing up. Because "nice" requires the slightest movement of mouth muscles into a smile and something as simple as "hello." Anyone unable to muster that is dealing with some serious garbage problems.

Oh God, here come the DMs. "My son has special needs and he can't make eye contact." "My daughter is agoraphobic . . ." Folks, do you really think I'm on a crusade against people with mental health issues? Do you really think I would write a whole paragraph on why someone with a disability should try harder when I meet them? As a rule, we are talking about the average person. There is no fun in going after someone at a disadvantage. Many stand-up specials ago, I had a joke about a girl who was chosen last at a bar at the end of the night. Not wanting to make the reason she'd be chosen last about anything women are actually judged for, like body type or looks, I gave her a whimsical twist. I had her say that she would sleep with the guy only if he would "let me wash my hump first." I picked a hump because it's not something you see outside of a fairy tale. Still, I had to field (and by "field" I mean accidentally open, mark as unread, and delete) a message from a woman *outraged* because her son has a hump. I don't know what to tell you guys; if you are willing to laugh at others but get really offended when it's about you . . . maybe don't watch anyone's stand-up or anything ever, then?

But I will tell you, in a normal social setting, the quickest way for me to dislike you is for you to deny me a proper greeting.

I was waiting in line to do the red carpet at an event a few years ago behind a model/actress/LA resident who, I promise, you have never heard of. I say that to reinforce that, while it's sadly tolerated when celebrities are assholes, it's especially obnoxious when someone thinks *trying to become* a celebrity *requires* being an asshole. A mutual acquaintance introduced us: "Iliiiiiiza!!!!!! Do you know Gloryhole?" (I've named her Gloryhole for this story.) Smiling, I extended my hand for a friendly handshake. And then she too extended her hand into mine . . . and the moment we engaged in handshaking, she looked away. So now I'm just standing there, holding this woman's limp hand while she *pretends* to be busy looking around.

RAGE VOMIT! Who the hell is she trying to be? Nothing says, "You don't matter, and I'm wearing the *face* of a human, but I'm actually a barbarian," more than shaking someone's hand but simultaneously not acknowledging them. And, by the way, we were both *waiting* in the same red-carpet line . . . Clearly, we weren't outranking each other. I don't know what came over me, but I gripped her hand with both hands, like one of those sincere presidential handshakes, but firmer and with more of an agenda, which brought her attention back to me.

"I like to make eye contact when I meet someone," I told her, smiling. I always believe, in any situation, you should start out giving all people a basic modicum of respect (and, as they prove to be terrible, you may whittle that away until you are totally avoiding that person). You can tell it jarred her, because she immediately told a bad lie, brushing it off. "Oh, sorry, I have like, a *thing* with eye contact," she said, while making eye contact with me. And then she stepped onto the red carpet and made eye contact with every single camera and interviewer.

I have also noticed, particularly in LA, that people love to make their issues their identity. "I struggle with eye contact . . ."

"I'm weird about people." These are all generally code for "I'm an asshole, and I created a pass to give myself in case I feel like being rude as a way of feeling superior to someone because I'm not sure if they matter yet or if they're inferior in general which is why I am such a pill to be around."

But once we move beyond nice, that's when we start to run into issues. Because almost everyone can fart out a smile and a pleasantry. When you ask people to communicate, participate, and show up in a meaningful way, that's when you get to see what you're really dealing with. And that's when we all start bumping heads.

To quote George Costanza, "We live in a society!" And part of being in a society is knowing that your personal behavior, the second you leave your home, affects those around you. Literally no one cares how you act when you're alone.

Moreover, no one wants to know what you do when you're alone, what bizarre stuff you get off to, the boogers you pick, what weird accounts you scroll through, how much of a frozen pizza you can eat before realizing it was frozen, the sheer number of songs you make up about your dog, etc.

But we can't stay alone forever because humans crave interaction, we crave communing. We love to be around each other even if we aren't talking, and when someone else's bad behavior makes it difficult, it wrecks everything; our party is ruined. Birthday party, block party, after-party, dinner party, political party, whatever. Because this troublemaker has broken the tacit social contract that we are all supposed to act like people around other people! If you've ever been crop-dusted at a party, then you know what

I'm talking about. That person has broken the tacit social contract that we are all supposed to act like people, AND NOT DELIBERATELY FART ON EACH OTHER, WHICH I HAVE DONE MY BEST TO AVOID!

A few years ago, Noah and I were at an open house. We were walking around the primary bedroom, daydreaming about the life we would create for ourselves in this idyllic Spanish-style home, but our reverie was interrupted as the rancid smell of hot, angry diarrhea crashed over us. I swear some of the wallpaper started to peel off. We exited to the hallway to catch our breath (and see if any of the other open house–goers needed CPR) when we saw the culprit slink out from the en suite bathroom and rat-like scurry away down the stairs. The smell was so powerful that he must have eaten an entire wet burrito, washed it down with a cup of hot oil, and pulled over to fully unload when he saw the open house. Either way, he left the crime scene in that toilet and escaped and only Noah and I were left upstairs to field weird, accusatory glares from any prospective buyers ascending the staircase. I don't blame him for bolting, what was he supposed to do, stay and atone verbally to everyone who passed by? Actually, yes. He was. It was a NICE house! And there were civilians in there! We all signed up to see a house and be around other people, not get carpet bombed by airborne turd particles!

But we like being around other people. It's normal to want to socialize. I always feel bad for people who have the I LOVE CATS MORE THAN PEOPLE shirts, or mugs, or hats, because it just means people haven't been nice to them. We like who we like, and it's totally normal to only want to be around those specific people. If you're the kind of person who wants to be around people you hate and who hate you, then, well, you're probably a girl in her twenties with a tight-knit group of girlfriends. Or you're probably in show business.

> Now, if you are reading this from a self-created goat sanctuary in the middle of Idaho, then fine, yeah, you have chosen a different way of living that excludes interacting with people. But still, you will leave that goat sanctuary for goat supplies, and you're going to want the people at the goat store to like you so, at the very least, they are nice to you and maybe give you a discount on goat things.

But it's always important to remember to act like a person when you procure those goat things.

> "Act like a person" is something my mom says and a mantra I have carried with me well into adulthood. Even today I hear my mother's voice whenever someone is acting *off*. Not *off* in a way they can't help; not *off* in a way to suggest that their culture is different and therefore worse. *Off* as in being rude or unaware or gross, even though they know better. *Off* enough to need a reminder: "Hey, we're in this together; remember to act like a person." The statement itself presumes that a "person" is a being that upholds agreed-upon social decorum and would want to avoid having a negative effect on the person next to them. Like swinging your arms in a helicopter motion while walking down the street; that is not acting like a person. Or taking a lethal dump at an open house!

- The person blaring personal music in a public space. There's no way you are *actually* enjoying yourself with the song at that volume. Windows are rattling and birds are fleeing; my kidneys are vibrating. It doesn't make a guy look macho. No woman sees a guy in a doorless Jeep with subwoofers for a backseat and thinks, *Look how deaf he made himself go—let me in!*

- Owning a gun. I care less about you owning a gun and more about you discharging your firearm, at will, in a public place. Random vigilante justice isn't a dependable way to govern.

- The dragon exhaling a massive vape cloud upwind from you. You aren't cool; you aren't tough. What you *are* is addicted to nicotine and slowly killing yourself with electric puffs of Berry Blast and taking away my right to decide what goes in my lungs. You are trash, and you probably drink Gatorade with dinner. This also extends to the people who smoke cigarettes *next to* the door of a building. If it's cold outside, you aren't warmer because you are close to a closed door. You're just making nonsmokers walk through your smoke so you can shorten your journey back inside by about five feet.

- When your neighbor *refuses* to use trash bags, so their cans are overflowing with scoops of trash, like a garbage sundae, and the garbage flies all over your street, and you're like, "I can see the bag is from Nobu—how are you this dumb yet still make enough money to eat from Nobu so fucking often?! Three times a week? SAVE SOME FISH FOR THE OCEANS, GARBAGE CZAR! THERE ARE CROWS FIGHTING OVER KOBE BEEF! CROWS SHOULDN'T BE EATING COWS! IT'S UNHOLY!"

- People who ignite off-season fireworks. There is a special place for people who set off illegal fireworks in a residential neighborhood, and that place is hot and sparkly, and everyone is missing an eye.

The GREAT news is, from the poorest to the wealthiest person you know, everybody needs a little refresher on how to act like a person because, guess what, we really are all in this together and we're all capable of being good.

The idea of acting like a person speaks to the idea that we should all be better social neighbors, better at coexisting. It's the reason you cover your mouth when you sneeze, the reason you don't throw your trash in your neighbor's yard, the reason you use a turn signal. It's the reason you acknowledge someone by saying "thank you" instead of spitting in their face and yelling, "Bow to me!" We have elected to live around other humans, and therefore we have to remember that our actions affect those around us.

> I often take a brain-crushing six A.M. flight when I travel for work. It's early, and no one is happy to be there. Least of all the people who work on the plane. I always say good morning to the flight attendants. Maybe 10 percent of the time I get a good morning back or acknowledgment that I have said anything at all. And yes, it's a shitty feeling to toss a greeting into the abyss, but I still say it. Because you know what's worse? They're about to encounter a cavalcade of selfish flying monkeys who will blame the next three hours of their lives on them. These flight attendants are mentally preparing for battle. Either way, I don't let that define my choice to act like a person and say hi, because you never know how that little

acknowledgment might boost their mood. Also, if there ever happens to be an in-flight altercation or hostage situation, you want the crew on your side. It's insurance, really.

While we are talking about planes . . . I'm on planes more than the average person—how can I not talk about them? Air travel is an integral part of my career. Even if only one person isn't acting like a person on that plane, it could ruin the flight for everyone around them. Right? Middle seat taking up both armrests. People watching things on their tablets, volume up, WITHOUT HEADPHONES (is your dad the guy in the doorless Jeep?). The guy who stows his bag above the front seats even though he is sitting in the back of the plane (in case you don't know, this creates a luggage dam up top, and then no one in the front can put their bag away). A few years ago, I was flying home to Los Angeles from Las Vegas. And, hey, a Vegas-*back-to-LA* flight is always brutal. It's a plane of hangovers, blurry memories, and people flying away from mistakes and back to reality. Basically, once Las Vegas is done with you, even if you had a great time, there is no city you fly out of faster. The man sitting two rows in front of me smelled. This went beyond normal body odor. This was as if he had shit into his jeans, used the jeans to scrub his body, kept the jeans on for a workout, and then distressed the jeans with a razor made of hard, dry cat turds. It was so bad that the people around him called the flight attendant, and she had to ask him to exit the aircraft midflight. Kidding, we were still at the gate. For all the airline horror stories where a passenger becomes unruly or physically abusive, this guy was refreshingly compliant. He was way too accommodating about being kicked off, quickly getting up and grabbing his bag without an argument. Almost as if he conceded, "Yep, I know what this is about. Can't blame a guy for trying. Wanted to see how far I'd get smelling like rat mouth." Which leads me to believe this man boarded the plane knowing his smell was offensive and thought that if he could just get through the hour flight—at the expense of everyone else—he'd be able to get home, where the only shower in the world existed.

I (mentally) applauded him for exiting willingly, although I don't know how an air marshal would have handcuffed walking diarrhea.

People's inability to be considerate so consumes my thoughts and so repeatedly surprises me in new and horrific ways that I had originally thought of writing an entire book on how to act like a person. I wanted it to be like a modern-day Emily Post guide, but it felt tone-deaf, given how chaotic the world is lately . . . always was?

> I know I'm supposed to say that things were always crazy, and the Internet just makes everything seem worse . . . but things really do seem especially horrible lately.

One thing is certain in this life. No matter how much money someone has, no matter where they come from, who they are, how educated or uneducated, Instagram famous or *actually* famous to people over twenty-three—people everywhere, across the board, need help acting like people.

Self-reflection is a practice, and everyone is so afraid to give real-life, face-to-face, non-comments-section feedback. It's HARD to get the feedback that your behavior is rude or inappropriate in real time because no one wants to offend anyone, and, moreover, most people aren't invested enough in you to give you the courtesy of correcting you if you're being an asshole. They will just talk about you behind your back forever, like I did with Gloryhole.

I am not the arbiter of manners, nor do I care to always be the epitome of etiquette. I've been rude because I was in a bad mood. I've deliberately knocked into someone (who had it coming!). I will still eat with my elbows on the table, still say "fuck" at a black-tie event, and I don't say "God bless" or "bless you" when someone sneezes. Not only do I not have that authority, but it feels too religious and superstitious to be taken seriously.

For the most part, we are taught basic manners as children. But as adults, we often opt in and out of our manners depending on our feelings, our wants, the behavior of our peers, or just convenience. Maybe we are rude to convey power; maybe we are dismissive because we're insecure (eh, not maybe, absolutely). Maybe we don't know better, or maybe we forgot. Social expectations are ever changing (like, it would be weird if a man kissed my hand when he met me now . . . unless he was older, or Italian), but common decency is still mostly agreed upon.

I thought it would be fun to offer a guide on just a few things that I hold to be true. In these pages, you can privately question your own actions—"Oh, do I do that?"—and emerge from the pages 10 percent more like a person! Maybe even 50 percent. Oh my God, am I gonna win a Nobel Peace Prize?!

So let's start with something we have all done: visiting someone's home. I think given the self-imposed/government-mandated isolation a lot of us went through these last few pandemic years, a refresher is needed.

I'm not talking about dropping by a friend's house. I'm talking about a formal invitation. Drinks, a dinner party you weren't initially invited to but they realized you overheard them talking about it and it was weird to not invite you so they invited you, a coffee where you pretend to want to see their new baby, etc.

When you're invited to someone's home, you should bring a gift. Always. I don't know where the tradition comes from—I'm sure it has to do with dowry or avoiding a smiting from God—but the rule is sacrosanct. It's your way of saying, "Hey, I know you have spent time and money preparing an evening of food and/or drinking and/or group sex and/or games, and I see you have a little less money as a result. So I am doing what I can to make up for that. Here is a jar of Tostitos salsa I clearly got at 7-Eleven when I stopped to get gas. Here is a bottle of regifted prosecco that no one has ever wanted."

You should only ever bring what you can afford. There is no expectation that you should go broke to prove something. I always think something homemade is the best gift. When we sat shiva for my beloved dog Blanche (yes, we sat shiva and everyone took it very seriously despite me crying in pajama pants decorated with pictures of her face), my manager brought a glass carafe of home-made cold brew. Another friend brought oranges from their tree in a cute basket. As I'm writing this I'm realizing that 100 percent of the women brought food and drinks and only about 50 percent of the men brought food, and of those 50 percent I think 35 percent of them were in relationships and the woman actually procured the food. GUYS, YOU ARE PEOPLE TOO—ACT LIKE IT! AND IF I SEND AN E-VITE DO NOT TEXT/EMAIL ME A DAY BEFORE ASKING "Wait, when is your thing again?" CHECK YOUR INBOX, JOSH!

> I was once at a backyard BBQ, and a guy brought meat . . . but just for him. He brought a personal steak. The purpose of a BBQ is to get together and make food everyone eats, not to have use

of a communal grill for individual purposes—it's not a time-share. Meat is expensive, but hot dogs aren't. Chips aren't. Bring something for the people! That's so tacky, it's up there with bringing alcohol to a party for just you to drink. It's selfish and cheap, and you are for sure eating and drinking the things other people brought. And if you aren't? Why not just stay home FaceTiming someone while you eat a pork chop?

Even just a card that you write beforehand, preemptively thanking the host (while a little weird and I just sort of made it up), would be a very sweet thing to receive. "She wrote me a thank-you card for having her to my Halloween party . . ."

Whatever you bring, whatever you do, you don't want to convey that bringing the gift was an afterthought (even though it might have been) or an inconvenience (you had to bribe the Uber driver to wait while you ran into CVS).

However, if you are over thirty, it is unacceptable to bring something right from the grocery store, in its packaging, to the party. You want to stop at an Albertsons bakery and get something? Great! But if you show up to my home with a plastic container of generic cookies, price tag still affixed, it will be your last party with me! Put them on a plate! Presentation is nine-tenths of the law!

There are only two occasions when it is *maybe* okay not to bring a gift to a party.

The first is in your twenties when you go to one of those house parties being thrown by your college roommate's new roommate in a flophouse he's renting with five other dudes, and you're all gonna listen to music off a portable speaker, and drink warm vodka with no mixers until all that's left at midnight is, like, one handle of sweet vermouth because no one's sure how to drink it.

You *should* bring something because it's a *Stone Soup* situation, and if everyone brings a little you can all get wasted off cheap alcohol in red Solo cups with no ice. BUT since the hosts are a bunch of orangutans and it's a really drunken slopfest, not a food thing (because no one has money because you're all twenty-five and you're about to hook up with a guy who has a mattress and no box spring), it's okay to just show up with a six-pack of light beer. No one knows what's going on anyway, and when you're that young it doesn't matter what you drink.

> My biggest argument to the "we don't know what's in the vaccine" folks (who have hopefully decided to go along with science by the time this book comes out) is "remember what you were okay with drinking at twenty-three?" Yeah, roll up that sleeve.

The second exemption is if you go to a Really RICH person's party. Several years ago, when I was just getting started in comedy, I was invited to a big celebrity's house for a Fourth of July party/birthday party for one of his kids. It was deep in Malibu, so deep. Like, you would never find yourself there by accident, you'd have to be invited to go that deep. I was invited at the very last minute by a mutual friend, but I knew I'd be attending a birthday party, so I looked for somewhere that wasn't a grocery store to buy a gift. But it's Malibu, and aside from a shopping center on the way, there wasn't a ton. Not wanting to spend five hundred dollars on a pashmina or show up with an eleven-dollar bottle of Yellow Tail, I found a chocolate shoppe. The cheapest box? Fifty dollars. I still think that's steep! Even for Malibu! Especially for chocolate! I bought it, scribbled a little card, and went to the party. Once there, amid about a hundred people, I handed the chocolates off. I thought I had handed them to an assistant or a housekeeper. Frankly, I may as well have just thrown them into the ocean because I doubt the kid ever got them. Honestly, someone may have just left that party with a box of chocolates like, "Ooh, what a fun party favor." No one needed a box of chocolates, and they had the food situation covered with catering and the host had just told us the story of how he had rented an elephant as a prank on his wife. So, yeah, if someone is really wealthy and you're invited for something other than an intimate dinner, don't bring something that hurts your wallet, especially if the person you're gifting it to will never even know you were there. A homemade loaf of bread, flowers, a bottle of olive oil is fine. The real lesson is to plan ahead, always keep some sort of gift on hand that you can give, which that person can then accept and then regift. But don't bend over backward if your host owns a helicopter. No one cares, no one will know, and no one will remember. And you will be out fifty dollars! And I never got to meet that elephant!

Now that those polar-opposite experiences are out of the way, let's talk about how to act like a person at a party.

When I go to someone's home and they ask me to take my shoes off, like any normal woman, I always think of the restaurant scene in *Donnie Brasco* where they beat the Japanese restaurant owner who insists Donnie take off his shoes. Granted, this was a mobster with lingering WWII anti-Japanese sentiment, but still, people are protective over their comfort and belongings. We all remember in *Sex and the City* when Carrie (who was profoundly selfish—and I say that as a humble fan of the original series with every episode memorized [in place of baby knowledge]) didn't want to take off her beloved Manolos upon entering a friend's home. And, weirdly, a lot of men don't like taking their shoes off. I think it has to do with the primeval instinct to be ever prepared for battle. You can't fight an invading force in ankle socks.

But all of these people are wrong.

Someone is opening their home to you. Sure, they want you to be comfortable, but, more important, they don't want you bringing in dirt. They don't want your high heels making indents in their floors; they don't need your clodhoppers tracking in city filth. Are your feet *that* gross? Then you shouldn't be in sandals, and you should be wearing socks. And if you're in socks, then what is the problem, Stink Feet? You remove your hat (do people still do that?) when you enter a house, you remove your coat . . . so what's one more article of clothing?

If someone asks me to take my shoes off, I do it. No questions asked.

> Actually, if someone asks me to remove my shoes, my first thought is, *Okay, so . . . how cozy am I allowed to get?* It's a real *If You Give a Mouse a Cookie* situation with me. I will make myself right at home in your living room, with your snacks, on your couch, ensconced in your blankets, and then head into your kitchen . . . your medicine cabinet . . . Let me in your bathroom and I will touch all of your things and use a dab of all your creams and smell all of your oils. I wanna know you! I wanna be you!

Point is, it isn't infringing on your cultural rights to take off your Uggs, it's not hurting you, and you are a guest. Act like a person.

Gift giving is an interesting subject because a gift, no matter how bad, is still a good thing, in theory. At its best, the gifter feels great and the recipient is truly grateful. At its most mediocre, it's still a gesture that makes the gifter feel good even if the receiver thinks it's ugly. At its worst, it's a bad gift given in bad taste and the person receiving it doesn't want it and now everyone's a little resentful, but it still looks good that you gave it. Even though no one wanted it. No one's happy.

> There is a term for that, the act of something that neither party wants to do but you both do it out of a social obligation. *Arigata-meiwaku* (it's French. Kidding. It's Japanese, obviously): an act someone does for you that you didn't want to have them do and tried to avoid having them do, but they went ahead anyway, determined to do you a favor, and then things went wrong and caused you a lot of trouble, yet in the end social conventions required you to express gratitude.

Gift giving where everyone is being gracious and no one is happy? Feels like the cornerstone for a very WASPy Christmas.

> If you want to cringe-google and feel embarrassed for someone you don't know, go online and look up the time Björk assaulted a woman trying to give her flowers. (I think they were flowers; could have been a card or something. The truth is the video makes me so uncomfortable I couldn't google it for this story—I just had to go off memory.) She had just arrived by plane, and fans were waiting for her, and a woman extended some flowers, and Björk *snaps* and just starts hitting the woman. The gasps can be heard through the room; the deafening awkwardness created by this moment is one of the most uncomfortable things I've ever seen. And, like, what was that women's take-away? What if Björk had accidentally really hurt her? How do

you explain your wound? "I have this limp because I tried to hand Björk tulips at the arrivals terminal."

Anyway. Don't gift an orchid. We all know you got it at Trader Joe's, and, while it seems like a luxury item, you're essentially gifting a pot with a stick that will bloom for about a month twice a year. You are gifting a stick.

Don't bring flowers without a vase to a busy party.

I know you're thinking, *Is she serious? She's carping about a vase? People are dying!* Yeah, well, if you don't put them in a vase the flowers are also going to be dying (faster). So just do it.

As a host, the last thing you want to do is stop what you are doing, get out the stepladder, reach the top shelf, where you keep the empty vases, drug money, and Grandma's ashes, realize it isn't the right size, empty out Nana's urn, accidentally break it, ask your husband to look in another cabinet for the vase you were initially thinking of, get out that vase, realize it wasn't washed properly from the last use, wash it out, unwrap the wrapping from the flowers, cut the stems, put the flowers in the vase, dump in that included packet of flower food anthrax, arrange them so they don't look weird, clean up the stem nubs, throw away the plastic from the flowers, fill the vase with water, and then put it somewhere where everyone can see them but no one will knock into them, move it a few times, apologize to Nana, then get your guest a drink!

Bring the flowers already in a vase so the interaction can be clean and quick. Then it won't matter how ugly/carnation-y/daisy-y they are because they aren't a hassle.

A candle is the perfect gift (not for my mother, though!) for two reasons, none of which have to do with the recipient actually loving that particular candle.

The first being that the conceit is that almost everyone wants their home to smell lovely. Sure, there are some people who don't like fragrance, but, in general, most people like a nice smell. No one has ever smelled burnt hair and thought, *Man, I wish I could bottle that*. That being said, I do love the smell of gasoline and Pine Sol, but a gasoline candle feels like you're asking for trouble!

The question is, of course, "What is 'a nice smell'?" Because Yankee Candle Ocean Breeze might smell like the sea to you and like a bad lakeside Airbnb to me. Sicilian Lemon might remind you of your nonna's house or a Maggiano's men's room.

But that inherent difference in our taste of smell (what a weird phrase) is why the second reason is important. Because no one in the history of ever has ever been gifted a candle, sniffed it, and gone, "Are you fucking kidding me, Judy? On my *birthday*?! This smells like a rotting whale!" No. 100 percent of the time, people take a whiff, say they love it, and then either regift it or use it for a guest bathroom or to cover up a sewage pipe break. Either way, the gesture is what will be remembered, and you have acted like a person.

> Also, if someone gets you a gift off a registry, you have to write a thank-you note. Yes, you can fire off an email with your thumbs from your bed, but taking time to thank someone who took time with a modicum of civility shows a degree of polish I think we are sorely lacking in modern American society.

Sometimes acting like a person is ignoring another person. Since we agreed most humans are good, I think that also means most humans want to be helpful. But the other side of that is that most people don't actually want your input. You ever look back and shudder at a time you put yourself out there or volunteered information when no one really cared?

It is now almost seven years later, but every time I walk into a Starbucks, I think about that time I made a girl feel bad about buying a banana. I was at a Starbucks register and the girl ordering next to me had a lot of questions for the barista about sugar. She seemed concerned about her health, like she was struggling to make a "good" decision at the register.

> But also? No decision should be made at the register other than what form of payment to use. Apps, websites, investigative reporting, and posted menus—the information about the food is readily available. No order needs to be a game-time decision.

She had lots of questions about the sugar in the seasonal drinks. Which are basically just milkshakes with caramel drizzle, even if you make the "healthy" choice and don't get the whipped cream.

She ordered one and also grabbed a banana. Having heard her nutritional inquisition and wanting to help (but also demonstrate how knowledgeable I am because, to be honest, that's half the fun of doing a good deed), I chimed in, because she seemed so clueless: "A banana is like a sugar bomb."

> It's true! Bananas have potassium, sure. But that's all most people know about bananas, and, like, what does potassium do? Helps build the body of a banana? Helps with "recovery"? No one knows! Anyway, a banana can be over fourteen grams of sugar, which is a lot for a fruit that positions itself as a go-to

building block for protein shakes. It's also a lot of sugar for someone who seemed worried about eating too much sugar. I was expecting her to say, "Oh, really? Thank you for that information. You saved my life." She turned to me and said, "That's really rude. You don't know what people are dealing with health-wise." Knee-jerk reaction? I wanted to say "Um, I know you're at a Starbucks at Christmas choosing between a WINTER TRUFFLE BLITZ and a SANTA'S SACK EXPLOSION— it's not like you're in the ICU." But she was right.

Here I was, *thinking* I was acting like a person, but all I had done was offend her. She hadn't asked my opinion, she didn't need saving, and, for all she knew, I was a lunatic who had a lawsuit against Big Banana and this was a personal agenda issue. Regardless, everyone has opinions on food. And no one wants *your* opinion on *their* food. People get offended if you say their dinner looks gross; do you think they want to hear you tell them why what they're eating, in your opinion, is bad for them? No. No one wants unsolicited advice, no matter how good it is!

Not on what they should eat and not on their body.

Unless expressly asked, don't interject. That rule extends to asking women if they are pregnant, commenting on someone's size (not just weight—"You're pretty tall" is also mind-numbing feedback), or assuming someone doesn't take their health seriously. Chances are, they know, and chances are your commentary isn't coming from a place of real concern as much as it is something you said just because people feel they have to say something.

But perhaps this one banana was her only treat for the week, and I ruined it.

. . . But they aren't as healthy as people think!

HIGH-MAINTENANCE

I like to think of myself as low-maintenance. I also like to think of myself as a seductive French woman, and, depending how playful I'm feeling, I like to think of myself as a small cat with a song in my heart. How we think of ourselves and who we *actually* are don't always coincide. That's not a revelation. Have you ever met someone who says aphorisms like "good vibes only" and they're, like, *genuinely* terrible? Have you ever thought someone was normal but then saw on the news they killed someone? Have you ever wondered about women who try to cancel other feminists *in* the name of feminism? Have you ever had a friend who you know is a lunatic but all of their social media posts are about manifesting positivity? How many times has a guy described himself as an entrepreneur and, in reality, he just posts a bunch of memes about protein, "does sales," and DJs on the side? How many times have you said you're giving up meat but what you really meant was you aren't eating meat in between all the times you are eating meat? Don't we all talk about love and acceptance but sort of loathe most people?

I don't think I'm high-maintenance. The key is *thinking* you aren't. If you *say* you aren't high-maintenance (especially unprovoked), then you probably are. Falls under the Lady Doth category. Kind of like how the guys who always have to say "I'm a nice guy" are usually women haters? I . . . thought about a better way to say that, but yeah, no, I think that's apt.

I know I'm not high-maintenance, physically. But emotionally, I might require a little more external validation than, say, an accountant. I need thousands of people to laugh at me every night. I need to be told I'm doing a good job. One of the hardest parts of being in a movie is delivering a line and having the director say, "Cut. Okay, great, moving on to the next scene." It kills me. I NEED the praise. I need the instant validation. If the crew isn't laughing, then you're bombing, but they aren't allowed to laugh because it ruins the filming, but I neeeeed it.

Point is, there's the way we like to see ourselves, the projection of how we hope we are, and then the way we actually are. And neither is totally accurate. Everybody hopes they're perceived as perfectly as their curated social media accounts or whatever world they've set up in the metaverse.

But there is energy that goes into presenting oneself. It takes time and effort to simply exist and to exist in a way that you hope is impressing the right people.

Our society touts being low-maintenance as a virtue in women. It's seen as a positive because women have been told that no man wants a high-maintenance girl. Which isn't entirely true—no man wants a girl who is high-maintenance *and* kind of a nightmare. Plenty of guys have wives who require a lot of upkeep but who are loving. By the way, "upkeep" can be as menial as "She goes to Target three times a week and gets Starbucks every day." It isn't always about Botox in your elbows or diamond thongs or mink tampons.

But we've come to know "high-maintenance" to mean a woman requires a lot of physical upkeep and a lot of attention.

No one has ever said, "My wife demands we go to Home Depot every day! She's so high-maintenance."

And while it's easy to judge those women, I can't vilify them. Should you choose to participate in the expectation that women look a certain way (this expectation is perpetuated by social media and advertising, seldom enforced by a genuinely good guy), you're delusional if you think looking a certain way doesn't take time and money. So somewhere between the demand that a woman's hair be coifed, attitude be chill, eggs be ever ready, finances be in check (but not intimidating?), legs be cellulite-less, and vagina be the size and texture of a lamb's half-open eye, her face also has to be pretty with no makeup, her body hairless, her vibe malleable to every situation while still smiling . . . she's also not supposed to really put effort into any of these things? You are supposed to *naturally* be all of these things, and you are supposed to feel really bad if you aren't. I can't even call that gaslighting; I would just call it poisoning women's psyches. Dark armpits? You're the only one. Melasma and facial hair? Weird, no other girl has that . . . Irritated he asked you out at eight P.M. the same night he wanted to go out? You need to chilllll and just have some sex, be a cool girl!

Allegedly, guys like a grab-and-go. Pluck her off the shelf, throw her in the passenger seat of (insert truck type here), and head out for a sex-filled weekend of (insert type of trout here) fishing and her watching you play (insert game console here). This type of guy wants a chill girl who's naturally stunning, someone he can fit into his routine and his life and his choices and his pocket and she won't make too much fuss and will think burping is hilarious (it kind of is).

But I really believe that most guys don't care what their girlfriend or wife enjoys or does as long as she's cool to *them*. He doesn't need you to chug a Natty Light. He isn't trying to have sex with a bro with boobs. The TRUTH is men aren't paying attention 99 percent of the time to the stuff that makes your girl-world go around. Years ago, I used to occassionally wear clip-in hair extensions. My boyfriend at the time would tell me he liked it when I "wore my hair long." He didn't fully grasp that they were clip-ins. He thought I could just wear it long or short depending on what button I pressed on my head.

My husband loves me so much but knows that during the holidays, I'm busy putting up dead pine cones, cheap lights, and making the house smell like hot cinnamon! And I don't care if he likes it, and I don't care if he participates! Because he doesn't and he doesn't! But that's okay because I'm busy making COZY CHRISTMAS FOR OUR JEWISH FAMILY! And he's fine to not be part of that and let me do my own thing because it makes me feel good. Like how he doesn't come into the bathroom when I'm listening to deep house and ironing punk-rock patches onto my jacket.

Yes, I iron my jacket patches on in the bathroom! The floor is tile, so it can take the heat, and a woman's bathroom should be a personal oasis! I also eat snacks in there while I craft my jackets! And FaceTime my mom to tell her a story I've already told five people that day! It's my space! I would never call it my "lady cave" or a "she shed"—oh man, I've been wanting to tee off on this for a while. What woman has ever wanted to get away to a shed? WHY IS THE WOMAN IN A SHED? Sheds are for tools and horrible sexual experiences and spiders. I just loathe that because a guy has a "man cave" we needed to clap back with "We have a space, and it's alliterative! It's a SHE SHED!" Here's an idea: Share a fucking house like adults that don't hate each other. "She shed" sounds like you keep your mule of a wife in a shed. She has a shed, it's called THE REST OF THE HOUSE AND IT SMELLS LIKE HOT CINNAMON!

Your partner can still love you without loving the *same* things you do. I love *RuPaul's Drag Race*, and I'll watch it on the living room TV, and my husband will sit next to me, headphones on, and watch the Phoenix Suns play on his computer. Would I do the same for him? For sure. But, because we are sweet to each other, the second I need help with something, he's there. Men will do pretty much anything physical you ask them to do as long as you're nice about it. "Baby, it's raining fire outside, will you drag in the recycling bins and staple them to the roof?" He'll do it. No one wants to feel taken advantage of. Your boyfriend will go with you to a Sephora. He'll go into sleep mode while you shop, but he's fine to be there with you, at least for a little while. Because men like to be there for women. They like to help out, they like to feel needed.

Ever just felt terrible and cried in front of a male friend? They watch, and it's like a gorilla taking care of a kitten: They just want to hold you and aren't sure what to do and are a little afraid of accidentally hurting you. You want to see a person go into stun mode? Cry in front of a man you aren't sleeping with, like a good friend or a coworker. "There, there, little kitty. Cheer up—oops, I petted you too hard. I dented your head."

I think women who take *pride* in being high-maintenance often feel high-maintenance equals class equals self worth/being worthy of a man's time. The idea being "It takes money and time for me to look this way, and I look this way because I've been told I will have more value this way, and if you want to enjoy me for the way I look, you need to pay for it or at least accept that I am putting in this effort, and you need to just wait in your leased BMW 3 SERIES while I get it done if you want to have sex with me, RON!" I'm not a huge makeup wearer (I've had the same Benefit Hoola bronzer box for three years) and my clothes are usually limited to jeans and T-shirts. But I've never *once* been dressed and ready to go out before my husband. He throws on one of his six shirts and is *always* waiting for me by the time I clip-clop into the living room. "I just need to find my purse, have you seen my sunglasses? No. I'm tired. Should we bring water? Can you charge my phone? WAIT! I have to pee. Are you ready? Do you wanna bring the dog? Hold on, I have to change my shoes. Should we put shoes on the dog? Are you ready?" Through it all, he remains steady. Ever ready to leave. Me asking him if he's ready is, I guess, me projecting onto him that I wish to be ready.

> Women who take pride in and espouse being high-maintenance as a plus are usually doing it as a log line for a *Real Housewives* opening.

> "I'm expensive, and so are my divorces."
> *Spins around and smiles.*

> "They say money talks—well, I'm listening."
> *Answers a stack of money like a phone. Hilarious!*

"I killed someone with my car. I shouldn't be talking to you."
Puts on sunglasses.

"Diamonds are a girl's best friend, which is great, because people hate me."
Trips and falls into a well.

"'Business' is my middle name. Also, so is Janet."
Farts.

"Family comes first. I'll cum later, when I'm drunk and alone."
Cheers.

"Long hair, long nails, and a long list of hotels I'm no longer allowed in because of pending assault charges."
Makes cat claw motion.

"My mother was a bobcat."
Makes another cat claw motion.

"Money isn't everything, but have you ever had Kobe beef? So good."
Burps. Laughs.

"International waters are the perfect place to resolve a conflict."
Loads harpoon.

There is an emotional doubling down happening when women claim they love being high-maintenance or *love* being a bitch or a *diva*. I can't help but think they decided to lean into what should have been a fleeting name-calling incident. Maybe a guy once said, "You're too high-maintenance, and you are a cold bitch," and she was hurt by him and was like, "I've decided to turn my biggest problem into my greatest strength. I am MEGABITCH." To quote Eminem, "I am whatever you say I am." (Did I need to quote him?)

In theory, this can work. You can decide what your personality brand is and eventually people will accept it. "Sandra's a bitch; it's just how she is." "Derek is an asshole; it's just how he is." We all have that friend we've explained away to a new friend. "No, Kat has a good heart, they're just socially awkward and a little standoffish when you meet them." We have a lot of women on TV being self-proclaimed "divas," and that's just what their brand is, even if it's awful, even if they come off as insufferable. However, one thing I know is that most people are going to decide what you are based on who *they* are.

I've heard this feedback before: "A random guy said he met you after one of your shows and you were rude and kind of brushed him off." How is that even constructive? Like okay, next time I'll bring my blow job mat and try to make sure I give every single guy who looks at me a full prostate exam and bedtime story. Of the thousands of people I say hi to, somehow it's always the one guy who felt slighted whose story makes its way to me. Cool feedback, thanks. I'll make sure to change everything so you feel better about yourself.

I'm not *that* tough, but I come off that way to some people. Confidence coming from women is a hard thing to swallow. I've even had to check myself when I meet other girls and think, *Did I just write her off because she was actually rude OR simply because she wasn't smiling like a maniac and was just busy doing her own thing? Did I just fault her for the thing I get faulted for?*

But all you can do is be yourself; it really is all you can control. Trying to be something you're not is so exhausting . . .

I once tried to lean into the idea of being a "bad girl," and it went so, so wrong. I was in my late twenties, and I had had a crush on this guy named Mark for YEARS. I loved him. I loved him the way you can love a person whose birthday, hometown, address, and favorite color you don't know.

> You know those people who you've only had surface-level conversations with but you've had enough of them that you're pretty sure you would ignore every red flag they hurl at you just to be with them? I just thought he was so sexy, and all I wanted to do was put my body on his body. His body that I hadn't ever seen but, like, knew would be incredible. Or I was so into him that I never thought about his body and he could have had an iguana torso and I would have been fine with it.

I had a crush on him for years and then, one night, he finally asked me out. He lived on the west side, and I lived in Hollywood, and OF COURSE the date was by his place and not mine, but I didn't care. What's a few miles in traffic when everything you've ever wanted is on the line?! I brought my "date clothes" to a friend's house near his place so I could beat traffic, and then killed an hour before our date.

> Girls, don't do any of this. Don't drive to meet a guy near his place on a first date. Don't go so far that you have to consider rush hour and a pit stop to change. Don't put in any of this effort. This is so, so gross.

And the date was so, so boring. Had this happened later in life, I probably would have (never driven to a date and waited out traffic) bailed, but I couldn't help thinking, at the time, that maybe he was just nervous. Looking back, I don't think he was nervous as much as he maybe didn't really want to be on the date? Or worse, he was loving the date and thought it was a great idea to keep pulling me into bars to SHOW ME ART ON THE WALLS. I'm actively trying to get buzzed and sleep with you, why are you pulling me into some crowded bar on Abbot Kinney to show me the finish on the bricks in your friend's wine bar? Ugh, and we kept drinking wine, which I didn't like, and still don't love, really. I kept thinking, "I'm twenty-seven—where's the liquor, and when are we gonna kick this into high gear? If this guy shows me one more framed charcoal sketch of a horse . . ."

We *finally* got back to his place. I slid off my borrowed True Religion jeans, and when he undressed, I ignored his weird yin-yang tattoo from the nineties. And we started hooking up, and about fifteen minutes in, just as we were getting going . . .

I aCiDeNtAlLy BiT hiS PeNiS.

I didn't, like, *take a chunk out of it*. It wasn't even a nibble! Okay, I shouldn't have said "bit"; it wasn't a bite as much as teeth-on-skin *contact* and maybe some accidental pressure, but I can understand how he might have been upset. The second it happened, he RECOILED. Oh my God. Like, of all the things to happen when I'm trying to excite a man, him CRINGE-WINCING and sharply sucking through his teeth isn't part of the fantasy! I was trying to be sexy, but I also wasn't going for soft-biting his penis by accident! Blame the wine!

It gets worse.

In that moment, in that millisecond, I knew I had two options.

Option one: Be a normal human woman and say, "Oh, I'm so sorry," and try to not do that again. That's the option I'm pretty sure would come naturally to every person on earth.

There shouldn't even have been a second option! I hurt someone on their penis! I should have said sorry and moved on! The fact that in that nanosecond my mind saw a fork in the road is scary!

Option two: LEAN INTO THE MISTAKE. MAKE IT MY BRAND. It was a split-second decision, but I thought if I acted like I *meant* to do that, then maybe he would be turned on? Maybe it would come off like I knew his deepest desire? Maybe he'd be like, "Finally, the night has delivered me a Dark Queen, our pleasure is our pain! Only she understands the depths of my demons and can appreciate a good horse sketch!" It wasn't a *good* idea to pretend to be into it, it was just *an* idea. Like, could I psychologically frame it like I just *loved* pain and he should love it too? Could I make him think he was *actually* into something that is every man's literal worst nightmare? I went with option two and, in doing so, in that split second following his recoil, I DID IT AGAIN! Even as I write this sentence I'm yelling at my computer, "Why is no one stopping me?!" And I think when he, of course, recoiled again, I said something horrible I must have absorbed from watching too many movies with sexy female bad guys, like, "What's the matter, don't you like a little pain?" AM I A COMIC-BOOK VILLAIN?! *Don't you like a little pain?* I WAS IN STEVE MADDEN WEDGES AND A TANK TOP FROM EXPRESS! WHO WAS I TRYING TO BE WITH THAT LINE?!

Don't you like a little pain? He *definitely* did not.

Anyway. The night was pretty much over after that. But that was okay, we didn't have any chemistry at all. I couldn't be a sado-masochistic mistress of pain, and he couldn't be a man who loved having his penis tampered with. We both left that next morning being one degree more sure of who we were as people.

... Or. We already knew who we were. Years later, I ran into him while crossing a street in New York. We hugged and said hi and I think there's something sweet about the fact that neither of us ever told anyone that story. Or he told everyone and a lot of our mutual friends know I did that and I have no idea.

But anyway, being a woman *is* a high-maintenance job.

Let's say you want to be a functioning woman in our society: There is so much you must do. And I know, some of you will say, "Not me, I am to be a wild wolf woman who only leaves the den for necessities"—well, even a wolf woman has to think of things (vaginal care, sexual assault, lack of upper-body strength for timber hauling) that a wolf man doesn't.

The amount of maintenance a woman is willing to partake in varies, but let's look at an itemized receipt from head to toe, basic to expensive.

HEAD
- Hair: cut, blowout, color, straightening, perming, weave/extensions, wigs, wiglettes, mini-hats, micro-mini hat to go on the mini-hats, bows, specialty products.
- Brain: safety, doing twice the work for half the credit, other people's opinions affecting your reality, glass ceilings, being labeled competitive when all you're doing is being your best, being blamed for others being *intimidated* by you when all you're doing is your best. I can keep going, but if you really want to go through all the things women have to consider, just pick up my first book, *Girl Logic*.
- Unisex costs on top of that: Teeth and oral health in general.

BODY

- Clothes, clothes, clothes. SPF, moisturizer, makeup, tanning stuff, retinols, serums, oils, RX, peels, injections (Botox, filler, etc.), plastic surgery, Halloween mask to cover your mistakes, lotion, exercise, waxing, wardrobe, BRAS, shapewear, hose, heels, surgery from using most of these things wrong your whole life, body glitter, and the vast world of fitness!

- Vagina: tampons, pads, cups, waxing, yeast infections, prenatal appointments, abortions, any fertility help, the ticking clock of fertility, Plan B, Plan C, access to health care, UTI medicine, and general medical bills having to do with your uterus and the activities you partake in to unwind from in taking the mind-numbing amount of misinformation out there.

Every woman's routine involves one, several, or, unfortunately, ALL of these items to some degree. I'd say I partake in half these things. If I really stopped to think about all these things, like if I had to explain to a person who had never heard of the idea of gender or even a man all the things that "effortlessly" go into being a woman, I'd probably run out of breath before I made it to the shoulders.

What's incredible is how we undertake these obligations, how we fit all of this bullshit, both necessary and superfluous, into our lives, and yet, when a woman does these things imperfectly, we have little compassion.

ANNOYING COURT

Sometimes I annoy myself when I can't move as fast as I would like. Like, it used to be easy to just pick up and go; my life was a go bag. Keys, wallet, and phone. Go. Now I have to pee, all the time. I have to make sure I have my phone (which I should just break down and have surgically attached to my fucking eyeballs), my mask just in case (honestly? It's kind of gross to be in some places without one now), a phone charger, water (because GOD ONLY KNOWS HOW LONG I WILL BE out; what if I get caught in a sandstorm?!), Air-Pods, a set list, a snack, a jacket in case it's chilly, a hat in case it's hot . . . I do all these things so that I'm not caught off guard and annoying to others about how cold, out of touch, thirsty, etc., I am. (And, of course, bringing a baby is its own caravan of necessities.) So it is preventative. I do it for my loved ones!

But it's as if the universe senses I might be leaving my home and trying to have fun with my husband and it sends in an energy block. A PR nightmare in Santa Barbara, a ringing in my ear in Lake Arrowhead, a UTI almost anytime I have sex anywhere. WHY is there almost always an issue? I'm the first one to say suck it up and play through the pain. But sometimes it's as if the universe just *really* wants me to be uncomfortable. Does the average woman also have to deal with a romper always cutting into her vagina? Why do most of my shoes start to hurt only after I've walked in them outside of the home? Can anyone wear "nice" pants all night without them feeling too tight after dinner? Is there some ergonomic reason I can't get out of my car elegantly? It's always me coyote clawing at my purse and keys and phone, kicking the door open with a leg, and thrusting myself onto my feet. Have you ever had something bad happen and you don't have the ability to compartmentalize and you allow it to wreck your whole vacation?

> However, I did a month-long, thirteen-city stand-up tour through Europe at seven-months pregnancy. My husband was sick the entire time with some mystery cold and then got food poisoning. I didn't miss one workout, slept like a baby, and had endless energy. I was afraid I would give birth to a raisin because I was positive I was leaching off my baby's vitality.

Sometimes I just get so irritated with the way I can be. I think it's time I check in with myself by checking myself. I'm taking myself to court—annoying court.

Annoying Court is a minor court.

Disclaimer:

In order of civil importance it goes: Murder charges. Lawsuits. Moving traffic violations. Fashion court. Annoying court. You can be taken to annoying court by a relative, by a lover, or even yourself. It is the smallest of claims courts and there are no monies awarded.

I think all people should take themselves to court every few years to make sure they are self-aware.

INT. COURTROOM

Our hero, ILIZA (thirty-eight, thirty-four with a
lot of sleep, effortlessly gorgeous, doesn't know how
beautiful she is) takes the stand. Our JUDGE (always
a Black woman who doesn't suffer fools) gives her a
furtive glance.

         JUDGE
Mrs. Shlesinger—

         ILIZA
Whoa, you said it correctly—

         JUDGE
The charges being brought against you are that you're
an annoying person. You claim to be easygoing—

         ILIZA
Your honor, I *never* said I was easygoing. I claimed to
be low-maintenance.

The COURT REPORTER checks her stenography notes and
nods at the JUDGE

         COURT REPORTER
I think that's what she said. I have no idea what I've
been writing, these keys are all so weird.

         JUDGE
Nevertheless, today you are being charged with multiple
counts of being irritating on *several* vacations with
your husband. How do you plead?

         ILIZA
I feel like . . . I'm not guilty?

JUDGE
Counsel, you may proceed.

A LAWYER (sort of hot—but has bad shoes) approaches
the stand.

LAWYER
Ms. Shlesinger, is it true that in October of 2020 you
surprised your husband with a trip to Lake Arrowhead
under the auspices of "outdoor fun and then sex in a
tiny cabin"?

ILIZA
That is correct.

LAWYER
Is it also true that once you arrived, you claimed
your arm—let me read from the transcript: "hurts so
bad, I can't have sex, please kill me."

ILIZA
Well, yes, I had two herniated discs at the time and
the pain radiated down my left arm—

LAWYER
Probably shouldn't have taken the trip, then, huh?

ILIZA
It was nonrefundable. Also, I thought I had it under
control since the pain had been letting up. I think
the elevation of the mountains exacerbated it—

LAWYER
It also says here that you were "up at three A.M. with
a weird ringing in your ear."

ILIZA
Hasn't that ever happened to you? You're doing literally
nothing and your ear is randomly like, "Eeeeeeeeeee . . . "

LAWYER
We aren't talking about me—

ILIZA
"Eeeeeeeeeeeeee—"

LAWYER
Stop doing that!

ILIZA
I'm just showing you how annoying it was.

LAWYER
Yet you're the one on trial for being annoying.

ILIZA
Objection, Your Honor, he's badgering me.

JUDGE
You're on the stand; you can't object.

ILIZA
(*to her lawyer*)
Can you do something?

ILIZA'S LAWYER puts his phone away.

ILIZA'S LAWYER
Hmm? Sorry, I was chatting on Discord.

ILIZA
The *point* is, the ringing kept me up. I couldn't sleep.

LAWYER
Which is the reason, you claim, you were crabby the
next day.

ILIZA
I mean yeah, I'm not just, like, a *bitch*. I was tired.

LAWYER
Is a side effect of being tired having to pee ALL the
time?

ILIZA
(*sighs, resigned*)
No. That was because of a UTI.

LAWYER
This was only a forty-eight-hour trip. You must be the
least lucky woman in the world.

ILIZA
Yeah, well, having a vagina can be a pain in the ass.

LAWYER
And to cure this UTI you had your husband drive you—

ILIZA
I didn't *have* him. I *asked* him to drive me into town.

LAWYER
A half hour away?

ILIZA
Yeah? We were camping. Sorry we weren't Airbnbing *in* a
Walgreens.

LAWYER
So you could buy cranberry pills.

ILIZA
I mean, I was peeing every five minutes. It makes it
really hard to enjoy life. A UTI is—

LAWYER
Is this the same UTI you claimed to have in January
when you were in Big Sur and, again, had to drive into
town for pills—

ILIZA
I mean, no it wasn't *the same* infection, that would
be scary if I let it go that long. But yes, it was
another UTI—

LAWYER
Another UTI! Ladies and gentlemen of the jury—

ILIZA
There's no jury here and if there were, and there were
any women on it, they would understand—

LAWYER
If you had this many UTIs, wouldn't it make sense to
keep some pills on hand?

ILIZA
I DID! THEY MELTED IN MY BAG! And they crumbled all
over my toothbrush and I had to use my husband's
because mine was encrusted with cranberry gelcap crud!

LAWYER
So what you're saying is, you simply didn't plan properly.

ILIZA
Having a vagina should be an admissible defense of
literally anything! Would you be "cool" if you had
diarrhea every five minutes? Huh? Would you want
to have sex or be in a good mood or want to walk
literally at all?

ILIZA'S LAWYER stands up.

ILIZA'S LAWYER
The word "diarrhea" is hilarious.

ILIZA
(*to her lawyer*)
You're court-appointed, right? Like, I'm not paying you—

LAWYER
Your Honor, I'm merely building a case that this woman has been parading around under the guise of "low-maintenance," a "cool girl," a "fun wife," when, in fact, she has never gone out of town with her husband without bringing some sort of "issue" with her.

ILIZA
I AM FUN ON VACATION!

LAWYER
Totally something a fun person yells—

ILIZA
I don't *like* feeling annoying. I want to be carefree and be able to eat breakfast without taking a nap right after! I wanna stay in the sun all day, but I can't! I freckle!

LAWYER
Really? You don't like getting attention for your issues?

ILIZA
I stand alone on a stage for a living. I get plenty of attention.

LAWYER
I'm not sure you do, Mrs. Shlesinger. Two words. Santa Barbara.

ILIZA
That's not fair. I was being sued. I had done a stand-up show, and a "men's rights" group was suing me. It went on for three years! It was expensive and soul-sucking, and my lawyer called to talk to me on the first day of like the one vacation I was taking that year and—

LAWYER
It ruined your day—

ILIZA
YES! It's hard to enjoy an overpriced poolside club
sandwich when you know you're being sued! It gnaws at
you!

LAWYER
Must not have been fun for your husband.

ILIZA
No, but I'm pretty sure we still had sex.

LAWYER
Probably wasn't good, though—

ILIZA
The hell did you just say?

LAWYER
Moving on. A few years ago, you were playing in Houston?
And he came with you, it was your first trip as a
couple? He wanted to go out, but you picked a terrible
restaurant, and then you made him stay in with you
because your last book was due and you had to write?

ILIZA
He was *with* me on the road for stand-up. I can't help
if things come up. I had a deadline!

LAWYER
It was his birthday!

ILIZA
I got us room service!

LAWYER
He didn't like it!

ILIZA

Well, neither did I!

LAWYER

Your honeymoon?

ILIZA

I was jet-lagged! I had allergies! I was exhausted,
and I had just been overseas for two weeks working!

LAWYER

TOKYO?

ILIZA

Which time?

LAWYER

Both! You ruined both! But the second time!

ILIZA

OUR DOG HAD JUST DIED!

LAWYER

You stayed in the room crying. Your husband found the
strength to venture out and have dinner.

ILIZA

He is Italian! They use food to deal with pain!
(to her lawyer)
Are you gonna, like, say anything?

ILIZA'S LAWYER

Dunno, seems like you're kind of annoying on a trip.

JUDGE

I don't know, this whole case was sort of annoying and
a huge waste of time. I rule in favor of you, which is
simultaneously against you since they are charges you

have brought upon yourself. Sorry, what is it you want
me to do here?

    ILIZA
I didn't really want anyone's opinion, I just sort of
wanted people to listen to me.

    JUDGE
Granted. Case dismissed. There's ice cream and cake
for everyone outside!

    ILIZA
Because this isn't a real court!

The older you get, the more things come up. More years, more
annoyances, more details no one warned you about, more bullshit,
more doctor's visits. More days on this planet, more issues, more
quirks, more wrinkles, more eye rolls, fat rolls, ankle rolls. You
know those dreams you have where you, like, *cannot* get to class no
matter how hard you try? Either you keep running into an issue or
your legs don't work and it's one of those dreams that seems like it
takes hours to accomplish your objective? That's being an adult. It's
a long journey, you have a lot of things to carry. There is no right or
wrong way to balance it all. But a UTI makes it worse.

TRADITION

I've always been a little "anti" when it comes to trends. It isn't a hard stance: like a straight-edged, "fuck the establishment and everything it feeds us" outlook. I just don't like being force-fed things that I don't naturally find interesting, like hair coloring tutorials, gluttonous food influencer accounts/"What I eat in a day" montages, B-list celebrity gossip, anything about horoscopes, fashion hauls, and online spats that last for more than a day. Ya know, the *majority* of things on my social media feed.

But just because something is popular doesn't mean I'm automatically against it either. You know what's great? An Egg McMuffin. You know what's even better? Consuming one and a half Egg McMuffins (two will give you instant diarrhea) and six episodes of *The Big Bang Theory* on a commercial flight to Pittsburgh to play a corporate gig.

But that doesn't mean I don't keep it punk rock the other 99 percent of the time! Okay, 30 percent. And it's more suburban punk rock. Truthfully, I just listen to New Found Glory in my Volvo and talk about how people can fuck off, but I would never actually tell someone to fuck off, like, to their face. How gauche.

Would you? Honestly, when was the last time you *actually* did that in real life and not to a sibling over text? So, now I'll tell you, since we're keeping this honest? You're reading the opinion of a woman who thinks leg warmers with high heels went out of style too soon and who will still work "lit" into a sentence just for the sport of it.

What it really comes down to is that no matter how au courant you are, something popular can still be great, and no matter how "ordinary" you are, something that's popular can also be absolute trash. So with that said, here is a list of great things that just so happen to be extremely popular:

- Uggs: Ugly, yes, but also comfy! And cushy! And sturdy! And who cares if they don't turn men on? You want to call the women who wear them "basic"? Well, what makes the other women *so* complex? Huh? Are they wearing snorkeling fins in the snow reading Sartre? It doesn't matter—I'm never gonna stop wearing my Uggs. They are cozy and warm and make all women look like they have small bear feet from the calf down.

- Pumpkin Spice Latte references: In 2012, I put out my second Netflix special, *Freezing Hot*, and in it, I talked about Pumpkin Spice Lattes, commenting on the hysteria evoked when women realize that it's fall. I'm also pretty sure I even coined the phrase "Pumpkin everything"! Since then, PSL culture has taken over, so now, every September through December, I have to see PSL TIME embossed, stitched, woven, and drawn on every tea towel, tumbler, mug, and sassy personalized T-shirt from here to Etsy. The truth is, I've maybe had two of these drinks in my life. They are cloyingly sweet, taste nothing like Thanksgiving, and I can't finish a whole one without my teeth throbbing. But I do get why people lose their minds every year—they are comforting and sugar is addictive and IT'S FALL, MOTHERFUCKER! It's more the culture of being cozy; they evoke the idea of fall even if you're drinking one, sweating in a strip mall in Burbank. Also? Global warming is very real and I'm pretty sure we won't have fall one day, so enjoy it now. As it is in LA, we have to shop for pumpkins in 90-degree weather.

• Country music: It is great storytelling about the plight of the working man, the brokenhearted, and the hopeful, while also being anthemic for the people just really looking forward to getting bombed Friday through Sunday (everyone). It is a universal story, just told with simple harmonies and/or a banjo. The only reason to take a hard stance against it is that liberals are taught that people in the South do things like drive tractors to work and, oh, are also racist. We are taught, in sharing the ideas of open-mindedness that, essentially, rural culture is laughably foreign. Well, everything twenty miles outside of most cities is rural, and it's where all of your food comes from. You don't have to actually drive a truck to appreciate a man's love for his car (I sound like Hank Hill), and you don't have to speak with a twang to understand Carrie Underwood singing about vengefully destroying one.

Speaking of things that are popular, I have an additional list of things that *were* popular and have since fallen from grace, but I still think about them every day while biding my time until the trend wheel spins back around in their favor:

- Freestyle music: We're talking about the Cover Girls, Stevie B., Cynthia, etc. If you are over forty-five, Latino, or from Long Island, then this might be a very specific memory for you. Freestyle music consisted of two things: syncopated synthesizers and basic AB rhyme schemes about pledging your eternal love for someone you met at a club last night. I hear Stacey Q's "Two of Hearts" and in my mind I'm kissing some guy named Rocco behind a pizza joint in Queens in the late eighties. I was five in 1988. I've never been to Queens. Oh, the anemoia is strong with this genre. Look out, weekend, here I come!

  > For the record? I had to search to find a word that perfectly described the feeling I wanted to convey. "Anemoia." It's not in a normal dictionary, but it means nostalgia for a time you've never known. Great word, right? So fun.

- Hair feathers: These got popular right before Amazon Prime made shipping an entire kitchen overnight as easy as texting a dick pic to your mistress and losing half your money. Anyway, it used to take forever to get hair feathers. But there was something so bohemian and whimsical about festooning your hair with rooster plumage even though you had to special order them from a girl on Etsy who got them from her dad's bait-and-tackle shop.

- Glitter: Glitter on your face gave way to its more sophisticated cousin, highlighting. But I still think bedecking one's face with teeeeny shards of metal ensconced in a neon goop is the premier way to let others know you are ready to sweat. IT. *OUT* on the dance floor and/or mud field. Sure, it is/was bad for the environment, but then again, so is the paper on which this book is printed, and don't get me started on the harvested orangutan heart powering your Kindle right now.

- Hidden wedge sneakers: This is probably coming as a shock to many of you (in Oklahoma), but these are no longer in style. AND I MISS THEM. The comfort of a sneaker with the butt lift of a high heel? They were the perfect shoe for the stage, a high heel in sneaker's clothing, and I bought so many! Now I'm alone in my palace of Nike Sky His and, ahhh, they were so expensive, and I bought so many!

- Low-rise jeans (which I hear are coming back, but not for anyone my age. So more like coming back to haunt us.): When I was younger, I loved these because we thought only "nineties moms" wore high-waisted jeans. Abercrombie models would wear their jeans so low that the belt loops were actually just their pubic hair (JK, they probably didn't have any pubic hair). Now, of course, I do love high-waisted jeans, but they can be suffocating. I have a pair that starts at my ankle and zips just above my forehead (okay, it's actually an REI sleeping bag I wore during Covid). If you were too full, you never had to unbutton your low-rise jeans because your paunch would just pooch out and you could cover it with a billowy top from an airport Francesca's! For those of you too young to remember low-rise? It's the only type of shorts Britney Spears wears in her Insta posts. Google the television program *Rock of Love*, and you'll see more tanned, tattooed flank than you could ever dream of, and you might even see your mom! AH, I MISS THE 2000s! Okay, I think I might have mentioned *Rock of Love* in my last book too, but truth be told it's a goddamn cultural touchstone.

But then there are things that are so lame that won't leave our zeitgeist, and it's weird to me that they are so popular. My disdain for these things is more of a hard-core eye roll at things that stick around (SPIRITUAL GANGSTER shirts) for too long (unicorn-themed anything) and feminist-themed stocking stuffers. (You know there's a landfill somewhere filled with RBG resin pins and SLAY ALL DAY make up bags.) that I just don't want to think about anymore (that thing where guys fist bump and then make explosion noises). Look, I find a lot of things in our world annoying:

- LIVE, LAUGH, LOVE signs (or any words about praying, loving hard, lake culture, or positivity and gratitude painted on reclaimed wood). I get that there is finally a minor cultural backlash against words on décor/Rae Dunn–type art, but if you have only just now realized this stuff is absolute trash, then you may have been part of the epidemic. I've been rolling my eyes at this mediocre, often cheeky, religious-themed Americana garbage my entire life.
- How most eco-friendly products are either too expensive or just don't work well.
- How when people meet a dog they usually ask how much that dog weighs. Why? Are you gonna fight her?
- An impromptu piano performance from a random person in an otherwise quiet room.
- Papaya. It isn't good; I don't get it.
- People who tell you you just haven't had good papaya.
- The majority of America's inability to remove the idea of God from the quest for personal freedom. I don't care how many Bible quotes you use to support or deny abortion, gay rights, or your right to bear arms. The United States is a secular country. You may as well quote *The Joy of Cooking* to support your personal politics.
- Rapper feuds. *Real Housewives* feuds.

- Public Twitter fights where each person starts their retort with a crying-laughing emoji.
- "Nom nom."
- Late-in-life interest in photography (I am this person, and even I annoy myself with the amount of alley photos I take).
- Poodles. There, I said it. I especially don't like the big ones.
- Saying or writing: "baberz," "preg," "preggs," "preggo," "preggers," "hubs," or "wifey."
- Tempered excitement. It isn't *uncool* to be outwardly excited. It's not lame to have an emotion. You took the time to post a picture, only to write text that intentionally belies that happiness is annoying. I'm talking about people who post an accomplishment and rather than just be excited and say, "OH MY GOD, WE GOT MARRIED! I AM SO HAPPY!," they caption it, "We did a thing." Or that weird, unaffected language trend my generation started doing where when we wanted to post about friends or loved ones we would write "these two idiots" or a picture of a sunset with "ugh, this shit again."
- Preceding any occupation with the word "female."
- People who overuse the word "triggered."
- People who put a straw through the Starbucks sippy-cup lid.
- People who cite someone with a physical disability as a reason that anyone might need said straw as if that was ever who I was talking about in the first place.
- Giving a cat a deliberately long, Anglicized name like Mr. Snugglesworth Fluffbottom the III. (Part of that comes from being a comedian and always being on the lookout for things that are *hacky*. Saying, "I just threw up a little bit in my mouth," is hacky—as is the phrase "hot mess.")
- Wanderlust. You went to Tulum on a Groupon. Stop it.

- The mere mention of the consumption of rosé or pizza or tacos (or avocados, but I already mentioned that one) as a personality trait is passé. So many people have "I LOVE TACOS," "foodie" (ew), or "PIZZA GAL," like, *as* their bio. If you went in for a job interview, would you lead with, "Well, the first thing you need to know about me? I love a square pie!"? If that truly is a defining pillar of your existence, then put this book down and find a therapist.
- Calling something a "dumpster fire"? Also hacky. It's over, it's been done, and no one is still laughing. Please find new word combinations. Gabardine bobbery! There, those are two new words you've never seen together! "Myiasis" is another word you never hear. Don't look it up—it's gross.

The older I get, the more I find myself picking my head up from hypnotically drooling over my phone and exasperatedly blurting out, "Why are we doing this?!" More and more I begin to question things that are blindly accepted, but are actually just dumb.

MORE THINGS I DISLIKE:
- The automated printing of paper receipts, whether you want them or not. Have you ever tried telling a cashier that you don't want a receipt, just to watch them print it and then throw it away *for you*? Like that was the issue? As if your reason for not wanting it was that throwing it away would be too strenuous for you. I think of that receipt just being printed and saying, "Look out, world, here I—Oh!! MY LEGS! MY PAPER LEGS! WHY WAS I EVEN BORN?!"

- The oversexualized names of sushi rolls for white people (white men). "Sexy Roll," "Luv U Long Time Roll," "Two Lips Roll," and

"Sexy Bang Bang" were a few at this combo Japanese/Asian cuisine restaurant near my first apartment. I don't know who I feel worse for: generations of Asian women who have been sexualized because of ONE line in *Full Metal Jacket*, or the Oaxacan line cook in the back who has to read these sexual orders all day.

> The one line, "Me so horny, me love you long time," was said by a Vietnamese prostitute to two American soldiers in *Full Metal Jacket* and that line has been used as a catchphrase to sexualize and demean Asian women for over thirty years. Sex workers aren't perpetually horny; they are just trying to make a living. She wasn't turned on; she was doing what she had to do to eke out a few words in a foreign language and survive in a war-torn country, and it's actually really sad to think about. I guess that turns some guys on.

- The perennial deluge of oversized Bed Bath & Beyond coupons in your mailbox. Death, taxes, and BB&B mailers are the three unavoidable things in this life. Despite your having never shopped at one, one will find you and tell you about their never-ending 20 percent off sale. If everything is *always* 20 percent off, then it isn't a sale! Those are just your prices, Triple B!

- Automatically getting plastic utensils in your delivery order. This stuck in my craw, particularly during Covid. It shouldn't be a given that we just waste plastic because we are too lazy to think about it. Make the utensils fifty cents and allow people to opt in and out. We're all eating *at home*, where we have utensils. They get thrown in a drawer (we all have this drawer) with extra batteries and lighters and Bed Bath & Beyond coupons.

- Face-tuning/filters. Everyone rails against the *idea* of photo-shopping one's face, but most people continue to do it, hoping that, what? No one will eventually *see* them in real life? What's the endgame here? There are ten women who actually look like this in the world, and they are Russian and lucky. The rest of us are just lying our way through this alien cheekbone pageant.

- That one time a year when the town gathers and draws one name and whoever's name it is gets stoned to death. This one isn't an actual event, so much as it's the plot of the short story "The Lottery," written by Shirley Jackson in 1948. Here we are seventy years later, and this is our reality: just mindlessly turning on people, on our own allies, on our own idols. We attack people who had a public misstep, often don't give them a trial, and believe nothing short of them losing *everything* will be sufficient contrition. Tearing people apart because we feel so helpless has become the new normal.

It's hard. It's hard to stop what we are doing, take a look at it, and genuinely ask, "what am I doing this for?" If someone grabbed you while you were doing a remedial TikTok dance or smashed your phone while you half-asleep documented "What I eat in a day" and said, "WHAT THE FUCK ARE YOU *ACTUALLY* DOING?" and you had to genuinely answer? You'd be embarrassed. If you had to explain to a superior being visiting from space, or your grizzled grandfather, who went to war when he was eight, by saying, "Okay, so . . . there are these dances that appear on our phones and we, as adults, must repeat the dances and show the world that we have moderate control over our limbs and a vague concept of the beat. We get hearts if we do it juuuuussst sexually enough that we can still feign innocence. Kiss kiss. Tongue stick out. Winky baby!"

But that question, "What am I doing this for?," is one I constantly ask myself. When I post something or tell a joke, I think, *Is this genuine or performative? Do I stand by this? Would I die on this hill?* In addition to always asking myself, *Why am I doing this?* I often find myself asking, *Why are* they *doing this?*

I feel this way about getting holiday mail from mass corporations. Like, *who* is this actually for? The corporation doesn't care, and you'd have to be a serial killer to hang a card from them on your mantel. "We here at Mazda of Sun Coast want to wish you and your family/dog/tomato plant a happy holiday, MR. SAMVEL AKZARIAN (the last owners of my house never provided a forwarding address).

I also think that a lot of holidays are limply celebrated, without anyone getting any true joy from them. St. Patrick's Day, for example, was fun when I was younger, but I don't want to pretend to like whiskey and go on a crusty bar crawl anymore. Also, kelly green is exhausting to look at. And while we're on the subject of performative holiday routines? I absolutely abhor the texts from loose acquaintances wishing you a Merry Christmas or a "Happy Everything!" (Ugh, pick a side!) I know this sounds like a total Scrooge thing to mock ("And she was just so salty about people reaching out to say hello, women should never be annoyed, how unbecoming!"), but I have a finely tuned subtext radar, and I believe there is an agenda lurking behind that projected merriment in a mass holiday text. I think it comes from my twenties . . .

You see, when a chunk of my Elder Millennial generation moved to LA (to chase our dreams and age prematurely in the smog and sun while making sure most of our taxes disappeared deep into the crevices of local bureaucracy), we shared an unspoken bond over the fear of leaving LA. "Gotta stick around in case show business suddenly notices me and the industry calls, even though I'm twenty-three, work in an office, and only do stand-up in empty bars."

> Embarrassing side note: When I was about twenty-two, pre-iPhone (weird), there used to be a restaurant on La Cienega called Newsroom Cafe, and they had a computer in the waiting area for public use, and, while waiting to be seated, I pulled up a picture of my headshot and set it as the home screen of that computer. This would have been looked at as a brilliant move if anyone ever cared, or it had ever made a difference in my career. But what was an agent gonna say, "Wow, is that her OWN light brunette hair that she cut *herself*? Find her! Find this beauty! Make her the new Batman!"

We were afraid to leave town, afraid to loosen our (delusional) grip on the outcome of our future if we returned home for a holiday. But we would all eventually go visit home, and, desperate for a connection to someone back in Los Angeles (or lonely being in Los Angeles while your friends were gone), we (was it just me?) would send these mass texts wishing people a happy holiday. We would send them to friends and anyone more famous than us whose number we happened to have. The subtext and agenda being, "Please think of me! Please write back to me and let me know I still matter. Let me know I'm not alone in the universe while I toil away in the obscurity of my parents' suburban jail! See me! Just give me a quick hit of validation so I can go back to watching *Mrs. Doubtfire* in the den with my cousins and not feel like I'm totally out of the game!"

This is the textual tap—the SMS equivalent of a wave. Just letting you know, "I'm here and it will make me feel a little less anxious about being away from the rat race if a more valuable rat takes time to say hi back!" I never want to make someone feel like they don't matter, and I know the feeling on the other end, but I will say this: It physically pains me to have to write back, and you should know that making me take the time to validate you, a person I see twice a year, merely so *I* don't seem rude, makes me like you less! Is me writing "u 2 :)" fourteen hours later really driving home the holiday spirit?

Arigata-meiwaku! Remember? From the other chapter? That Japanese term that means everyone is trying but no one is happy?

My husband also shares my disdain for most trends, for sheepy behavior. He takes it a step further. The man owns almost only black T-shirts and won't wear anything out of the house with a logo on it. He owns one nice flannel and one sweater with a tiny hole. I try to dress him, but, and I know there are many women for whom this will resonate, getting my husband to try on clothes is like breaking a wild horse. The horse husband always wins because the stakes are higher for him as he fights, hoof and nail (so hoof and hoof), for his freedom. Our fashion sessions usually end with me defeated, folding another pair of slim-fit chinos back into their box and clucking, "Fine, wear black tube socks and that one pair of *dark denim* Levis to the grave, dress like a middle-aged lesbian, I don't care."

But recently our twin-minded reluctance and ability to question tradition came in very handy.

On Christmas Day, we ordered Chinese food. We did it a full day in advance because the world was knee-deep in Covid and anything last-minute would be sold-out, and anything decent would be a plastic-wrapped, tepid, half simulation of something that was once good, but that was still the best option. When you've been sheltering in place for almost a year with nothing to show for it beyond rapidly rising mortality rates in your city, the only real comfort is food and the safari you go on to procure it. While I realize so many people order Chinese food on Christmas, making it a sheepy thing to do, in this case I defend it because we are Jewish. It's a *Jewish* Christmas tradition. We did it first.

> Jews started eating Chinese food originally because, as immigrants in New York City in the nineteenth century, the two groups lived right next to each other. Historically, while gentiles were having their lunch after church on Sundays, Jews would go eat Chinese because it gave them a safe place to be, a place to eat, and, since the Chinese don't cook with a lot of dairy, there was less of a chance of mixing milk and meat, so it was close to kosher. Anyway, now it's sort of just the thing a lot of people do—they go for Chinese on Christmas. I wish Christians would co-opt some other Jewish traditions instead. Come hang out with us on Yom Kippur! You get to not eat for a day and apologize to people! You wanna hear air piercingly forced through a ram's horn to welcome the New Year? Right this way! Toooodleeeeee!

So we ordered it early. On Christmas Day, we drove from Hollywood to Pasadena to pick it up. Pandemic or not, Christmas in Los Angeles is bliss. For about two weeks, you get to experience a calmer Los Angeles and see what it would be like if it were a normal city, rather than a hot, pulsating urban rummage sale.

Due to all this, it was just a thirty-minute drive (which in normal LA traffic translates to about three dog years). We arrived to find about twenty-five people (masked, thanks to science, restaurant policy, and necessary public shaming) hovering around the entrance waiting on their orders. The whole purpose of pickup food orders in a pandemic is to not be around people, and yet, everywhere you went was like *28 Days Later*: just exhausted people idling, unaware of how close they are to each other, moaning under their, often half-mast, masks. And we were no better!

It was only after we waited twenty minutes that the ersatz unofficial Covid officer/security guard/restaurant host/whipping boy reluctantly admitted to us, the unwashed waiting masses, that they were running "about two hours behind."

He related that some of their staff had called out last-minute and they couldn't get shifts covered on Christmas. So people continued to wait, on a packed sidewalk, for upwards of two hours, to get their preordered Chinese takeout.

During Covid and in its wake, there was this tacit understanding that you're going to use a portion of your disposable income to "support a local business" (and then you would post about it, to make sure everyone knew what a good person you were . . . for getting takeout), and your feedback is irrelevant because they are doing the best they can amid an impossible situation in which they were completely abandoned by their government during a world health pandemic that absolutely decimated a nine-hundred-billion-dollar restaurant industry employing nearly fourteen million people. So it's a nightmare for everyone.

But we had a realization, canceled our order, and left. The realization was not that we were angry at an understaffed restaurant running two hours behind on takeout orders on Christmas Day—it was that we were idiots for trying to get food from one of the busiest Chinese restaurants in Los Angeles on the busiest Chinese takeout day of the year. I was so annoyed with myself for not thinking about it, and just *sheeping* along. And I didn't even care about the tradition that much. The truth is, Christmas Day means nothing to me, and what I eat in general means even less.

> My husband is a chef, and he has saved me from a life of bagged deli meat and crackers (JK, I still get 'em in, I've been snacking on them since page five), but I'm not a food *enthusiast*. I will also do anything to avoid the lengthy conversation with people where they insist they're "easy" but then slowly realize the menu is a land mine. Aside from octopus, which I won't eat because I think it's a bad idea to eat your eventual alien overlords, I'm a selective omnivore, if that's a thing. You wanna go vegan? I'll hamster nibble with you. You wanna do all meat? Great, I have a few sharp teeth left. You wanna just "do heavy apps and a cheese plate"? It would be my second one of the day, but sure. I'll eat whatever, just please, please don't tell me about your diet. Oh, what's that? You have that weird genetic thing where you eat cilantro and it tastes like soap? No, I actually already knew that because you tell me about it *literally* every time I ever eat with you. So . . . I am no *foodie* (blah!). I can appreciate a farmers' market tomato, but I still think Twizzlers make great straws.

Other than being a little hungry for longer than I would like, nothing happened. I didn't grow claws; my intestines didn't bottom out—we were *fine*. I looked at my husband and I said, "You're a chef; let's just go home and get drunk and (you can) cook pasta. We can eat Chinese food literally any other day of our lives, forever." So we went home and the world kept turning and we ate tasty pasta, got buzzed, and fell asleep at eight thirty. We didn't even get Chinese food the next day, because it wasn't that big of a deal and who wants to drive to Pasadena twice? It's a half hour away! THAT IS SIX DOG YEARS.

Christmas, spiritually, religiously, doesn't mean that much to me, but holidays are many things to many people: joyous, expensive, obligatory, fear-inducing, and socially pressurized. However, there are only a few that get the full commercialist/capitalist treatment, right? Christmas and Valentine's Day, of course, come to mind as days where you have the most societal pressure to engage (or *get* engaged, am I right, *ladies*?! Okay, that's my set!), but not all holidays command your attention like those do. When's the last time you bought trees for Tu BiShvat or baked bread for Lammas Day or threw up on St. Barfy's Eve?

But in the world of peer-pressure-infused celebrating, New Year's Eve is the greatest offender, because you always pay more and get less. At its best it's a glitter-covered, prix fixe, upcharged hot flash of a forced gathering that ends with a cheap champagne toast in a plastic cup. At its worst, it's still that same sentence except someone also dies on the ride home.

> I want to be clear: I am up for being financially taken advantage of, but in a fun way. We all sign that agreement when we buy anything that isn't a no-frills necessity, like a Costco pallet of toothpaste or health insurance, that we will be paying a fee for a little bit of luxury. When you buy almost anything, the vast majority of the cost is in the name that's attached to the brand, versus what you're actually receiving: a bag of chips (it's mostly air), fancy lotion (it's mostly water), or Nikes (ooh, they're imported from China, how exotic!). A Supreme shirt is basically

a white-labeled Gildan tee with an iron-on patch—it's the shirt a radio station would give away at a car dealership promo event.

But I will go along for the ride if it makes me feel special! Cue the sheep noise! (You can hear me do it if you buy this book on Audible.) Charge me more for face cream, just make sure the model pushing it is impossibly exotic so that I'll think using it will make me look like a lithe, freckled, Afro-Asian twenty-year-old. Charge me double because it came from a curated monochromatic Instagram account that also shares positivity aphorisms ("You be you!" Click link in bio to figure out how!). Tell me it has some buzzworthy ingredient I have a vague understanding of, like Cordyceps. They're healthy, right?! Which is better, chaga or Reiki? How much matcha is too much matcha? Or should I switch to maca? Is it appropriation to even say these words? Which one is in this nine-dollar probiotic CBD latte? Which one will make me the youngest?! Give it all to me! And sort of lie to me, I love it. Tell me they *may possibly* contain *potential* antiaging properties that *could* reduce the *appearance* of *some* fine lines *if* applied every day forever! Serve me previously frozen, farm-raised shrimp from Thailand but serve it with an incredible view of the ocean! Book me a boutique hotel so exquisite (one that has a sundries shop that sells something super necessary, like handcrafted leather AirPod cases and mugs that say edgy things like **bitch juice**) that they make it easy to forget an omelet is the cost of a mortgage payment. You ever check into an Ace Hotel? They are not cheap, but the front desk people are pretty! And cool! And are the kind of people dating apps use to lure you in and then you never see them on the actual app. There is a guitar in your room and a record player you can pretend to care about! That's value!

Still in the pandemic, we wanted to just avoid New Year's Eve entirely and get away somewhere. But when I went to look up "Covid-friendly cozy getaways" (you have to use the search word "luxury"; otherwise, you will end up renting a raccoon crawl space in someone's duplex because it was written up as "cozy," a key word *they* used to fool *you*), like camping, house rental, RVs, a plank drifting out to sea, nothing was available. There was nary a yurt unoccupied for five-hundred miles north, south, or east of Los Angeles. While Noah and I were quarantining, missing holidays, and staying in as much as possible for the cause, people were clandestinely booking up every hidey-hole and rat bed from here to Tahoe. And now I wanted a rat bed and they were all taken! I did actually see one Airbnb that looked incredible, and it was . . . down the street from me. Then we applied some of our Chinese/non-sheep-brain restaurant logic to the situation. Why were we racing to vacation during the only time other people had to vacation? I'm a comic, and Noah is a chef, so we're used to operating during off-hours, when other people are sleeping or working. We can get drunk on a Monday night, nap pretty much anytime before six P.M., or, in this case, just go on a vacation the Monday after a holiday weekend.

What was the rush? Why are we paying extra money just to be somewhere at midnight when we were going to be alone together at midnight anyway? Why? So someone can scroll past a picture of us kissing and then finger-grunt out a "like"? 2020 wasn't even *worth* toasting good-bye, and 2021 was going need to fill out a job application before I got my hopes up about its qualifications, so what the hell were we doing?

I was still writing this book in at the end of 2021 and I didn't get why we were celebrating a new year going into 2022. Had we learned nothing last three years? At the very least, we should be bracing for whatever's ahead, not blindly celebrating its arrival. The earth orbited the sun, it's a planetary movement, not a cosmic guarantee that things will be better. I'm afraid we might have to . . . learn from past mistakes and actually work toward the year we think we deserve. And since this is coming out Fall 2022, I hope we did? Probably not? I hope you aren't reading this from a *Waterworld* floating garbage island.

What makes holidays special is other people, the warmth of your friends and family, and doing cocaine with that one cousin who was always too young for you to really hang out with but now that she's twenty-five it's like you're the same age. I thought, what if *I* *saved* the money from that New Year's Eve upcharge and booked us a getaway a few days *after* New Year's? The resort will be even emptier, and the rooms won't be as expensive. It was the perfect plan. It's not like anyone gets any work done that first week back anyway. It's just a lot of creaky "Hey, just getting back and settled in"—*Yawwwns, sips tea*)—"I didn't have a chance to read any-thing you sent me in the last two months (because I forgot but also didn't want to). I'm gonna put a pin in this, munch it over, circle back, squeeze the beaver, and I'll close the loop ASAP!" In my industry (actual show business some days, animal wrangling and pest control others), most people are lazy. I'm sure this is true for every industry, because most people are lazy, but about 10 percent of Hollywood is actually creative. The other 80 percent are: terrified of losing their jobs because of a creative mistake, are only allowed to say no to things, and have "some notes about your female protagonist's likability in her own book of essays." You thought I did the math wrong and you are wondering about the other 10 percent? They're dead. They died in the Fox lot trying to get out of the parking structure.

I had booked our getaway for early January at a resort on a massive property where each room is its own freestanding structure, i.e., socially distanced, no contact with anyone.

I was so excited to be lucky enough, in a pandemic, to be able to get away. After a year of hard road work touring outdoors, then no touring at all, over two-hundred episodes of a weekly cooking show, both of us getting Covid, a miscarriage, two herniated discs, and the general anxiety that comes with your city, state, country, and planet being in a health crisis . . . it was going to be nice to just take a break in a way that ceaselessly refreshing my Instagram couldn't provide me. I wanted to be together in a beautiful place and just take a breather. That's all that mattered. What also mattered was that just outside our room, I got to see a banana slug and six *fully* antlered deer eat grass and I took a bunch of blurry pictures that no one ever will want to see. Also, I fed (threw) a dried apricot to the main deer, and I like to think that was very special for him. Maybe it will become our tradition. Probably not. Deer don't live that long.

UNPLUGGING
(A CONTINUATION OF THE LAST CHAPTER
BUT WITH A DIFFERENT TITLE)

We booked our stay for four days. Three is more than enough, but the truth is, I don't take a lot of proper vacations (just another way to add an item to the annoying court docket!), and I am really bad at relaxing. *But, Iliza,* you might think, *you seem so calm when you're running around onstage, sweating out rants at two-thousand words per minute!* I know, hard to believe.

I'm not high-strung, but I'm not . . . What's the opposite of high-strung? A relaxed pile of strings strewn into the shape of a mandala? I am not a chill person. I know it's not cool to admit that. I'm supposed to say, "I'm chill about whateva, whateva, and it'll all work out, good vibezzz only." Yeah, it'll all work out because I'm forcing it to! And even if that isn't working, the mere act of attempting to force it makes me feel like I'm being proactive (i.e., writing this book proposal on the vacation I'm about to tell you about), even if I'm just proverbially treading water. You may not get anywhere treading water, but you are building endurance and muscle, which you will need for when you finally do get goin'! But yeah, no, I'm not chill. I get worked up over small things. I am constantly rehearsing lines for a confrontational conversation I'll never have, and if I can find a rabbit hole to bore deep into about a hypothetical something that will never happen? I will fling myself down it. I have no major hobbies and no interests outside of my all-encompassing job, and, honestly, I like it that way. I work out so I look good for my jobs on-screen and because the endorphins from my workout sometimes are the only good feeling I can create for myself in this thankless, trying, endless gauntlet of a career that I love! I read books and watch TV to stay sharp, keep up with the world, and remain sane (not a requirement for being in entertainment, just a *personal settings* preference). The rest of the time I am literally *doing* my jobs. I do not want to do other things. I do not want to take up candle making with harp seals or miniature kitchen design for gerbils. The rest of the time? I'm with my baby, Noah, or one of my three close friends or I am sleeping. I sleep about nine hours a night, and I can go even longer if the room is really dark and my husband doesn't breathe.

So I booked an extra day because, to be honest, sometimes you need extra time for your brain to adjust to being on vacation.

Fully surrendering to the tranquility of a vacation is like slipping into a really hot bath—you need to do it slowly so you can acclimate and not burn your butthole and vagina. No one just *jumps* into a hot bath; if they do it's probably part of some experimental therapy or a cult initiation.

I spent an inordinate amount of time deliberating between writing "butthole *and* vagina" or "butthole and vagina or penis," but the truth is it's probably mostly women who will read this book and everyone has a butthole and if you don't have a vagina I don't think you're going to stop reading based on one decision and say, "She lost me; she didn't include the mention of a penis and this has become totally unrelatable." Anyway, the point is, I decided not to go with "bugina."

All I'm saying is the extra day creates just a little bit of a mental runway. A mental vacation to get ready for the physical vacation. You may roll your eyes at that, but if you've ever had a cocktail on your way to Vegas, crammed a complimentary in-lobby welcome dessert into your mouth, or raised a glass in an airport Applebee's (the guy cheersing you back is *never* hot) and said, "Fuck it, I'm on vacation," then you know what I'm talking about.

Noah and I decided to turn our phones off. I told my assistant that if anyone I loved (not just, like, a random celebrity) died, she could call the front desk to tell me. We left our Chinese rescue dog, Tian Fu, with my mother-in-law, Nancy, who is a saint.

However, there's always an unspoken . . . I wouldn't call it a *tension*, but a teeeeny elephant in the room. It's a key-chain-sized elephant. A few years ago my best friend/soul mate/beloved-by-all journey dog of nine years, Blanche, died while Noah was with me on tour in Japan. Did she die in Nancy's house while Nancy was out? Yes. Was it Nancy's fault? No. Was Blanche maybe secretly old and everyone but me could tell because I only saw the heavens when I gazed upon her face? Yes. Was that phone call she made to us in Japan to tell us Blanche was dead one of the hardest things Nancy has ever had to do? Probably.

Probably? I don't know. I really should ask her more about her life. But probably. And while it was horrific to have my dog pass away when I was half a world away and at work, I think it would have been worse to have her die unexpectedly, like, *in* my bed or like, *as* I was deep kissing her. The fact that it happened on Nancy's watch and not mine is something I choose to look at as a cosmic favor. Nancy took an emotional bullet for me that day, and I'll never forget it. Anyway, when we leave Tian Fu with her, I always have to tell Nancy, "If Tian Fu dies while we're gone . . . don't tell us till we get back. It ruins the trip, and if she's dead, there isn't a lot we can do."

The last time we were at this resort was our honeymoon in 2018, and WE. DID. DRUGS. I put that part in caps in case you are reading this and thinking of giving the book to your kid, so you can cross this part out. Or don't. It's not like we did heroin. That's in chapter 12.

Here is the thing that no one is talking about: Almost everyone is doing drugs all the time. And if you do them responsibly, they can be awesome. Bad things in moderation are super fun, like being a bitch or dating a hot idiot.

Now, I don't want to have a conversation about this in real life. I'm not a drug enthusiast, and they aren't part of my "lifestyle." My brother is a cannabis farmer, and, as much as I want to be into it, I just don't like pot. And do not give me that, "Oh, you just haven't had the *right* weed." I'm almost forty, I went to a liberal arts college, and I live in California. I've had my chances. "No way, you just need some Purple Norcal Indica Giblet Rum Tum Tugger." Nope. I'm good. If I smoke weed, I think about death 100 percent of the time. I actually *enjoy* clinging to reality. I think weed should be legal and taxed and regulated, just like sex work should be. But I don't want to partake in either of them. I want you to have it if you want it and want to pay for it. Just quit blowin' your shitty blunt smoke in my face.

We got these pills as a wedding gift: a capsule of powdered shrooms with pure MDMA lightly peppered in. The last time we took them, it was like I dipped my brain in a serotonin bucket then tucked it into a nice warm bed made of, well, I was gonna say something cozy, but it's a brain so, blood. A bed of blood! So cozy for my brain! Blood Bath & Beyond! Here's a 20 percent off coupon!

When I say to do drugs responsibly, I mean that more about the way *in which* one does them. Obviously, being addicted to something is never good (*Sets down phone, stops scrolling through TikTok*). But there is a way to do some drugs and not be sloppy about it.

THE THINGS YOU CAN DO TO GUARANTEE YOU HAVE A WEIRD TRIP

Do mushrooms indoors: Bad plan. They are natural and should be done in nature. But when you do them outside and marvel at our planet, please try to avoid the phrase, "Nature is putting on a show for us."

Have aggressive, loud, sad, or shitty music playing: You don't wanna feel like you're trapped at a bad party with no ride home. That being said? I once had on Vanilla Fudge's "You Keep Me Hangin' On" during a trip and it was, I'm not exaggerating, the best two minutes of my life. Okay, thirty minutes—I had it on repeat and didn't realize it.

Be around someone who you aren't 100 percent comfortable with: If they have a weird vibe when you're sober, that vibe is gonna be even weirder when you can see their soul.

On our honeymoon, we did drugs the adult way. We got up, had breakfast, worked out, and then took them dead sober in the middle of the day. Then we went on a beautiful walk and marveled at an incredible creature (which, it turned out, was just a rabbit with really long ears). Later that night, I had a tasty root beer and a few bites of soup, and I woke up the next day feeling totally fine. People usually feel like shit the next day because they drank all night, depleted their seretonin, sweated out their electrolytes, and exhausted themselves.

The thing about drugs is you can never have the same trip twice. Each time *can* be incredible, but it will always be different. Different conclusions reached, different feelings tapped into, different things you write down then revisit when you're sober and you're like, "What the hell does 'kindness is all of it' mean?"

So this time, again, we took the same kind of pills and went on our walk, all bundled up and ready to be toasty and high in a beautiful forest. But it wasn't kicking in. And as the late morning sun beat down on us, the walk got very hot very fast, and, somehow, the hills on the hike were steeper than last time. I was sweating through my (sort of useless but cute) fingerless wool gloves. We got back to the room, I tore off all my layers and just lay on the couch, sweating. I started to get annoyed because the drugs weren't working, my stomach had been bothering me (because I was thirty-seven, and why should any day ever be pain-free again?), and I was *abnormally* tired. I was so annoyed by being so let down, and I started tumbling down that angry rabbit hole I spend so much time in that it's basically like a second home. I started to mutter to myself, "Of course you pay a resort fee to carve out a fucking break and this is what you get. You should have just stayed home and refreshed your Instagram feed and obsessed over ticket sales or something." But I pulled myself out. I remembered the Chinese food, and I thought, *Even if the drugs never work, you're still in this beautiful place with Noah and you can still relax; you're probably just tired because you've finally "given yourself permission"*—*Rolls eyes so hard, pulls eye muscle*—*to unclench your jaw for five fucking minutes*. That's what I told myself. I told myself that's why I was tired.

Then Noah started to feel really good: His pill had kicked in. He was happy, blissed out, sitting on the balcony and staring out at nature. I thought I was getting there but, uh-oh . . . rumbly tummy.

> Something about magic mushrooms always makes me poop. I mean, when you do them you are, in effect, lightly poisoning yourself, so it makes sense that they might disagree with you.

I went into the bathroom, naked and phoneless, and sat on the toilet. *Weird*, I thought, *has the porcelain always felt this relaxingly cool?* Or was I just hot? And THAT'S when the drugs hit. While I was naked, on the toilet. I was rolling on the toilet!

> It was, and I say this without caring that I'm a woman typing about defecating . . . THE SINGLE GREATEST POOP ANYONE HAS EVER HAD OR EVER WILL HAVE. Poop? Shit? You *have* a poop; you *take* a shit. Either way, I did it. I had and I took! The

best poop of my life; the best poop of anyone's life. Your dad spends a lot of time on the toilet? All of his greatest shits combined (and you know he's ranked them) don't add up to a plop's worth of what I had! You know how great it feels to take a huge dump? You do, admit it, Madison. Now multiply *that* times however many nerve endings are in your butthole to the power of being chemically incapable of having a bad thought. That was my dump. You know at the end of *Raiders of the Lost Ark* when they open the Ark and all the spirits fly out and melt the Nazis' faces off? *That feeling* but, like, fun.

I finished my business and drifted back to the bedroom, each step a discovery of movement and the unsung joys of walking on carpet! I curled up on the bed. Even though I felt *incredible*, I kept yawning; it was a little distracting for me. I wanted to do some deep thinking about life, but instead of that, I was in a ball, feeling the pure energy of every molecule of my being, and ceaselessly yawning, like an exhausted Cheshire cat. I spent the next hour intermittently taking five-to-ten-minute naps, waking up to smile at Noah enjoying himself on the balcony before I'd slink back off into sleep. I was just *so* tired, and when the drugs wore off, I spent the rest of the day and night just exhausted. Why, oh, why was I so tired?

I know right now you're thinking that I'm about to reveal a medical diagnosis. Please shelf your expectations. The stakes of this story are about to get incredibly low.

I woke up the next morning feeling great, and I went to take my WOMEN'S ONE-A-DAY FRUITY CHEWY ADULT CANDY FUN-TIME CARNIVAL MULTIVITAMIN (WITH IRON). Then

I noticed I had extra. I realized that I had extra, not because I'd packed too many vitamins, but because, and this is the dumbest thing ever, my *melatonin* is also FRUITY CHEWY ADULT CANDY FUN-TIME, and I had put them all in a bottle *together*, and I'd taken TWENTY FUCKING MILLIGRAMS OF MELATONIN that morning instead of my vitamin. Twenty milligrams?! That's enough to kill a horse if the horse was already really sick and one inch tall! So that explains why I was so tired. It had nothing to do with, like, "giving myself permission to exhale" or whatever. It was me overdosing on melatonin fruit salad pills.

When the vacation was over (and I had stopped mainlining fruit-flavored sleep aids), I had had my phone off for three days. With each passing minute I was getting closer and closer to becoming a Zen, unplugged, unaffected embodiment of tranquility; a positive intention incarnate; a walking yoga mat. I knew that when I left this magical place, my friends would remark, "You seem so different now, so centered," and I would inhale deeply and say, "It's just that 'kindness is all of it,' ya know?" Then I would disappear into a puff of turmeric and gua sha movements . . . and Cordyceps.

You'd think the universe would reward you for being so good. The universe would say, "You unplugged for a soft seventy-two hours (I checked a few things when I got up to pee at night because I also had a UTI! So fun!), and in that time all the things you were waiting on happened. Nothing will ever upset you again. You are fulfilled and successful now, you've been nominated for the Most Grounded Human of All Time Award, and all of the E-list celebrities you wrote 'happy holidayze' to in 2007 got back to you."

But there was no reward in store for me. No huge uptick in follow-ers (people often unfollow when you have a serious opinion that differs from theirs, so you would think that if you post nothing, people would flock to the stillness!). But no. Instagram, the virtual garden I so lovingly tend to, had nothing new for me. Shockingly, the world continued to turn regardless of how little I checked in or participated.

A total of three five-day-late "Happy New Year" texts from num-bers I had never bothered to save were waiting for me. Someone texting you "happy" anything five days late doesn't warrant imme-diate reciprocation.

> Plus, we know how it will go: I'll text something deliberately casual back like "HNY," my brevity implying and hopefully con-veying how reluctant I am to participate. And a day later they'll "heart" it and ask, "How's life?" or worse, "How's LA?" Who has ever given a satisfying answer to that? How's a whole city?! What kind of an impersonal, unanswerable vacuous question is that? "How's LA?" How is your *entire* family? How's world health? How's space?! And then I'll say, not sure how heavy they want me to get about Los Angeles, eschewing any authenticity, "GREAT LOL," laughing at literally nothing. Then they'll ask about something randomly personally granular like, "Is your sketch show coming back?" and then I (still not knowing who this per-son is but we've been corresponding since 2017 and I've never put their name in my phone and I don't want to scroll back far enough to try to figure it out) have to admit (what I've known since the day it aired) that it isn't coming back. Then I issue a preemptive strike of a text to avoid their feigned, yet obligatory, pity by immediately typing, "But oh well, onward!" and then they

send me a strong-arm emoji, and then we don't text again until the next holiday, St. Barfy's Day. And I'll never know who they are.

I turned my phone on, and I felt nothing. Not joy, not validation. Not a warm, digital embrace. Not a calmness as I waded back into the choppy, pukey waters of social media. I think I felt slightly annoyed, which is my stasis anyway. I checked my emails. The majority of them were from people apologizing for "not getting back to you before the holiday," aka people who took *their* time to unplug and "are just now seeing this email."

LIES. You saw it, you just didn't care!

I don't believe in setting up an auto-response personal away message on my email. My parents, my assistant, and my manager know I'm gone, and that's really all that matters. If your company makes you post one because you have clients reaching out, I get that. But a personal one is just a self-important e-brag. You may be on vacation, but you will be checking your email at some point. Fiber-optic cables make up 90 percent of the rainforest canopy. There is cell service in the Mariana Trench. Dunkin' has free Wi-Fi *in* their coffee. WHERE THERE IS A WILL TO CHECK EMAIL, THERE IS A WAY, EVEN IF YOU SAY YOU ARE AWAY! No one knew I had unplugged because no one *needed* to know. I wasn't launching into space; I didn't need to *bid farewell* to my circle. No one knew I had been gone, and no one noticed. Which is how it should be—people should be living their lives, not monitoring someone else's. Sure, there were 90 percent *fewer* dog pictures posted to Instagram in those days I was gone, but still, no one noticed I was gone. Okay, I had a few panicked texts from my best friend Greg saying, "Where are you?" Then ten hours later, "I'm worried," so it was a mistake not to tell him since we talk every day. Oops.

And then it happened: I logged on and the first thing I read was that a bunch of deeply stupid, misled, and violent terrorists had broken into our nation's capitol: self-proclaimed patriots who had sought to upend the very foundation they claimed to be fighting for. It wouldn't have mattered how Zen I was in turning my phone on, or how centered I was. As an American, as a true patriot, and as a fucking human, it rattled me to my core. I'm glad it did, because it meant I cared. I immediately threw myself into responding, into posting what was pouring out of me. Truthfully, more often than not it's a futile exercise that does nothing but preach to your own choir and lose you followers. But I couldn't help myself.

And this wasn't the first time I had become this way. It wasn't the first time I'd let my blood boil and taken on a fight no one had asked me to. Sometimes, some causes are just so all-encompassing that if you say nothing, you are complicit. For your own soul, for your own mental health, you have to express yourself. Screaming into the wind has become the only way to hope to be heard these last few years.

I was hopeless, angry, and nauseous. You think, *Turn the phone off; what is so important?* And the answer is everything. Everything is "so" important, and things don't stop being important or scary just because you don't hear about them immediately. And they also don't stop happening just because you aren't seeing them. In retrospect, I probably couldn't have stopped a coup at the Capitol from my house with my Instagram account. And carving out four days to give yourself a break is okay. Carving out any time to give yourself a break is okay, because as much as we all feel the weight of the world is on our shoulders and everyone is waiting for our reaction, it isn't and they aren't. You know how many career-altering internet fights could have been avoided if one side just never commented back? And, if you can just not respond, the petulant online public usually moves on pretty quickly. It's all about how much you are willing to take on, knowing that no matter what you give, it will never be enough for the majority of people disagreeing with you, judging you.

The lesson I'd hoped for that week was learned after all—just not until a few days after I got home. After three days of gripping my phone, entrenched in angry DMs, shoulders up to my ears, fighting (online) for what I believed to be right, reading every article I could so that if some faceless stranger challenged me I would be armed with facts . . . I was more stressed than I was before we even took the trip. I felt horrible. My face was hot, my phone was overheated, and my neck was throbbing. 99 percent of the engagement was positive, but, as a true comic knows, you always have to focus on the one guy not laughing. In this case, that "one guy" was several hundred people who either unfollowed me or told me how horrible I was for not supporting an angry horde of turncoats. I lost one thousand followers that day because I took the time to tell people that I was upset that a guy in a Camp Auschwitz shirt was part of a racist mob who broke into our capitol. Sometimes it's really hard to fight for a country that wishes so many of its citizens were dead.

I stood over the garbage unwrapping individual chocolates, stress-eating fifteen of them, just hoping the chemical reaction from the sugar would be an instant panacea. Okay, I ate twenty. And I don't even like chocolate.

But I like people, and I like conversations. I really believe that if you can talk to someone without attacking them (or without them *feeling* attacked) and without them feeling embarrassed, they're more likely to be open to a kernel of a new idea. I like that my comedy brings people together who are miles apart on a ballot—and I hate when I lose followers like this, with them refusing to even think that they might be hurting people. They left without knowing my heart, without knowing that I'm the kind of person who believes in a gray area and abhors absolutism. Were they all racist anti-Semites? No. Were some? Definitely. Did I wish they would stay? I don't know, I guess I'd like to think I can change people.

> I think my fear of being unseen and unheard and feeling like I led an unremarkable life that impacted no one is what drives me to do stand-up. I just figured that out as I was typing this.

We don't allow for nuance in anything; we are a nation of cancel buttons, sweeping generalizations, fear, and outrage. And we all think that everyone else is the problem.

I wanted to make nice; I wanted to post something unifying. I went to post a simple picture of the American flag, but for every sentence I constructed, I could already see the angry responses from both sides of the political spectrum:

"Land of the free, home of the brave."

"Not all of us are free, you racist bitch."

"God bless America."

"Get your religion out of my face!" or "Nice try, you liberal fucking Jew."

"Never stop fighting for what you love."

"Are you inciting a riot?" Or "That's why we stormed the Capitol, you fucking snowflake!"

I felt then as I often feel: that I couldn't say anything without being misconstrued, misunderstood, and mislabeled. It was paralyzing. The distilled anxiety made my blood feel sour. Every thought was negative; every breath was short.

I couldn't believe that I wasn't able to figure out a simple sentence about my country out of a genuine fear of how loud other people's ignorance could be. And here's the kicker—no one had even asked me to post anything! This was all self-inflicted because I was allowing it! I was so disappointed in myself, at my inability to compartmentalize this anger, that I kept allowing this to upset me. It's not like I was a senator and my campaign manager was tapping her foot: "The *Times* needs a statement—we gotta give them something!" It was one o'clock on a Friday, the sun was shining, I didn't need to be doing this, to be feeling this way.

But that *need* to say *something* remained. It always will. I'm a comedian, and I'm a writer. It's what I do: I observe, and I comment. So I simply posted the American flag, and I wrote, "I love you." I wrote it because it was true, in the way a mother loves their child who shows serial killer tendencies and bites his teachers but is a sweet boy when she tucks him in. She loves him because he's her blood. I posted the flag, desperate for people to say nice things in the spirit of shared patriotism. The first comment I saw was from a private account (of course, all brave people fire from behind a wall) saying something to the extent of "Oh, *now* you're a patriot?" Implying I had only recently decided I loved this country and had done nothing for it prior. Indignation seeped out of my sweat glands when I reread that sentence. And then another woman wrote, "Cute. Where were *you* during BLM?!" My stomach did a backflip into my throat.

Those two people were clearly from different sides, but what they both had in common was they were angry and could take it out on me. I erased my flag. I think I posted something about my new haircut instead, just to clear the bad energy. And the flow of my comments section immediately ran positive again. People only interact with your posts as they feed into their feed, and no one really looks at your static posts in the context of your life's work or your work's ethos. No one would notice that I had taken down the flag and instead posted about my stupid fucking haircut (which did look awesome).

The issue isn't that things are crazy and people are crazy. What's crazy is that I'm still surprised by this. The issue is how much I (particularly as a woman who dares to try) allow it to rob me of joy and drive *me* crazy. I made fun of the "asking for permission" idea but, even as a strong woman, I do it. And it does help to have someone in my corner, validating me with "Yes, nobody cares if you go to sleep and live in a tree for a week, you deserve it. #bathbomb."

Years ago, for years, me and my (other) best friend Jodi, a hilarious comedian, would call each other to ask, "It's okay that I canceled my set tonight, right?" We were women who got up and did shows *every night* (eh, usually not Mondays—who goes to a comedy show on a Monday? Probably the same person who jumps into a hot bath) and of course we were entitled to a break, but always had trouble taking it. The reason could have been feeling sick or deflated, or even just wanting to spend the entire evening on a date, and not bolt out halfway through appetizers to play for thirty people in an attic.

I used to schedule my dates around my stand-up. I'd schedule a dinner date for ten P.M. so I could do my sets first and get them out of the way. I'd do my hair and makeup at home, do shows in jeans and a T-shirt, then change in the comedy club bathroom into my "date outfit" (usually the same jeans but with a tank top and heels) and meet up with him. You know what makes you feel like a transient pack rat? Carrying your clothes and shoes around in your purse all night.

And yet, to us, the idea of not putting in face time for our fifteen-minute spots was crippling. We would always validate the other one: "Oh my God, of *course* it's okay, nobody cares and it's a shit lineup tonight anyway." Deep down we knew it was irrational, and even deeper down we believed the advice for the other person but never for ourselves.

When you're in the thick of it, in the rat race, fighting to be seen, the idea of sitting down, of *unplugging*, so you can recharge and start back up stronger is so hard to grasp. I would come home off four nights on the road and sign right back up for local shows that next day. If I didn't, someone else would get that spot. And then I thought I'd be forgotten forevaaahh.

Did the dedication pay off? Of course it did, but I'm sure I could have spared myself a lot of stress, a lot of angry emails to my manager, and a lot of beating myself up. I could have done it with more grace, and I still have the chance to.

And here we are, years later, and none of those nights we canceled mattered. Well, one did: It was the night I decided to go on a date with a man named Noah.

> My show was actually at a bar, and, after we saw a movie, I told Noah I had a set and he decided to come along. Then we got drunk and then we got married. But not all in one night. But yes, my husband came to a show on our first date.

People don't know you and your everyday struggles. They don't know the shit you put up with at work, how much your foot hurts, how scared you are for your community, the issues with your parakeet's beak health, or the litany of hurdles you jumped through today and the rest of your life just to simply be. And to be fair, I don't know what those people who write mean comments are going through either—whether it's a sick parent, a cheating spouse, or an acute, irreversible case of their head actually being a whole, flaccid penis. People will always casually say, "You do you, take time for yourself." But only you know when you really need a rest and, rather than get sick (ooooh, and so thin) and exasperated, and I can only say this from years of pushing myself: Give yourself more breaks. Give other people more breaks. That doesn't mean be lazy; that doesn't mean lose sight of your goals. And it doesn't mean don't chime in when there is something to be said. It just means . . . in the end, you can only control yourself. You are the only one in charge of how you are going to feel; no one else really cares. Have more snacks, more treats, more naps, and less writing back to people who don't deserve a response. I can actually say that I make great efforts to be kind enough to myself because a less anxious me is a better wife, daughter, friend, and comedian (and hopefully mother). Oh, and also author. I feel like this book was really fun for both of us!

LEGAL FORTY

I do not resent aging. So far.

I know, any woman over forty read that and is letting out an Ursula-like laugh. "Oh, my darling, just you wait, you'll see!" And I understand that. It's easy to say you don't resent aging when you don't fully feel the effects of being "older" yet. Nothing will make my eyes roll out of my head faster than hearing a younger person talk about how much they have figured out.

I remember a friend's friend talking about this guy she was dating who, based on his haircut, I knew was trash. A high, tight fade with long hair flopped over on top. You've seen that guy's Instagram. It's a lot of him in unbuttoned flannel with thick metal jewelry posing in a barn. He used to be a youth pastor but now he's a "brand ambassador who dabbles in stand-up." I remember her saying she loved him and they spent every weekend together, but he didn't want to be serious, so she wrote it off. "I'm just gonna keep hanging out with him; we both like, really just want to enjoy each other for now and we don't care whether it turns into anything. I'm not in a rush. I have so much time." She was twenty-eight. I was thirty-five. I thought, *Oh, just you wait, you'll see! You are letting him waste your time! You poor unfortunate soullllllllll!*

In the words of twentieth-century Alabama philosopher Charles Barkley: "Father Time is undefeated."

What I resent is not being allowed to revel in these last glowing years of my thirties because everyone rounds your late thirties up to "almost forty." Which is basically forty. It's forty.

At thirty-eight, to the world, you are forty. So what's the point of actually *being* forty if we are *accusing* you of almost being forty for the last few years of your thirties? Why? I guess because forty could practically be fifty, which, in Instagram years, is basically dead. But what's the point of numbers if each one doesn't hold a value? 1 + 1 = 2, not "2 and sorta 3 because 2 is so close to 3" . . . No, that logic only applies in the ever-nebulous world of bra sizes.

As my husband always says, "Age is just a number . . . that tells you how old you are." You aren't a legal adult until you are exactly eighteen. You aren't legally allowed to drink until you are exactly twenty-one. So we should be calling it a "legal forty." Legal forty isn't thirty-nine just like seventeen isn't a legal adult. No matter how much of an "old soul" she is. Normalize #legal40.

Your thirties should be a chef's tasting menu of years: several small courses, each with its own inherent specificities.

YOUR EARLY THIRTIES (thirty to thirty-four; thirty-five if you moisturize)

College is starting to feel like another lifetime. Your sights are set on real things like a home you don't share with people you aren't related to or maybe getting married. Depending on your city, you might still have roommates, and you are hopefully beginning your ascent into the upper echelons of your job. You can still be considered a *rock star* at work due to your youth and ability. You're still young enough for miniskirts, but you're starting to feel like the big kid on the Forever 21 playground. Maybe you consider yourself a wine drinker now. You're also keenly aware that you will never be on a "thirty under thirty" list.

Men in their twenties are starting to call you old, but men in their forties are suddenly looking attractive to you. They are still a little old, but not gross. Women in their late thirties don't take you seriously. You might still be on your parents' cell phone plan.

YOUR MIDTHIRTIES (we'll say thirty-five to thirty-six)

This is when your career starts to really take shape. This is also when you might quit said career, pump fake and go to grad school, or start a TikTok about the "refurbished van you drove across the country." You are also starting to panic about being thirty-five, because people keep saying you are almost forty, and you are really starting to measure yourself against literally anyone who has anything you don't have. If you aren't married, you are starting to feel left out. If you are married without kids and wanting them, you are starting to feel left out. If you are married with children, then you are . . . probably from, like, anywhere that isn't Los Angeles or Manhattan. And maybe you are missing being single and without kids.

YOUR MID- to MID-LATE THIRTIES (it's literally thirty-six to thirty-seven)

I know I should have more advice on this, but I'm a road comic: I was somewhere between Iowa and England for most of this, and then I got married. My advice? Buy property, set up your IRA. Apply hyaluronic acid, and start doing neck stretches.

YOUR LATER MIDTHIRTIES (thirty-seven until 39 years, 364 days, and 23 hours)

These years are spent being keenly aware of how close you are to forty, but you still feel far enough away. You might experience your clothes being a tad tighter than they once were. Seemingly overnight, it's as if you've lost the ability to drink alcohol and feel decent the next morning, and certain types of alcohol really start to disagree with you. You have the money for expensive face products, but you kind of just always look tired, and, again, the bra you've had for years is a little tight: a condition I call "The Thickening." You don't even need to gain noticeable weight; it's more just a metabolic/body shift. You are a tad puffier than before, and, for the love of God, do not go upside down and see what your knees look like from that angle.

YOUR LATE THIRTIES (it's the hour right before you officially turn forty)

It's a beat. It's a moment. Your late thirties are when you are exactly thirty-nine years and twenty-three hours. But, technically, *turning* forty is still part of your thirties. Remember, the year 2000 was not the technical beginning of a new century; 2001 was the beginning. So, *technically* (based on Millennial science), forty-one is the beginning of your forties.

You are in one of three parties.

Party one: You are dreading turning forty because Hollywood has brainwashed women into thinking anyone over twenty-five is old and unlovable.

Historically, the male preference for younger women stemmed from the desire to further a bloodline, because younger women are more fertile. So initially, it had less to do with a learned preference and more to do with ancient reptilian survival tactics deeply embedded in the brain. But since people are living longer and women have more options for fertility as they age, the modern male desire to mate with a younger woman has less to do with procreation and more to do with ego. The idea that a man is capable of attracting someone younger means he is still seen as desirable. So it really has less to do with your age, ladies, and everything to do with his age, which reminds him that he is getting older and will one day die. That's why you feel "old," because you were told so, not because you are.

For your whole life there has been a buildup to this moment. Turning from a carriage into a rotting pumpkin, here you come.

Party two: You are ready to be forty and begin an incredible decade filled with a lot of the same stuff as before, but more expensive and with more prescription creams. And louder orgasms? You're ready to make "giving less of a shit" a full-on and to write it in glitter on your new journal. Also, you took up journaling.

Party three: You don't care; you aren't thinking about it really, and there's no point in loving it or hating it because it's happening. Like another *Fast and Furious* installation.

We all like to think we are in the third party, but we dabble in all of them, depending on our moods.

I believe the constant rounding up in age is only done to make people feel bad. Why are we always rounding up? I mean, we could play the age relativity game all day. Why stop at "almost forty"? I'm thirty-nine, but I'm also almost fifty if you compare me to a fifteen-year-old.

And it's never positive—"You're almost forty; you should still be able to wear cutoffs." It's always this subtext of "Get it together, you should know better, you're almost forty, put down that bottle of Aftershock Hot & Cool."

But how can that be? How can I be anything other than young? I feel fine (usually).

I can't be forty. I can't be thirty-nine. I'm supposed to be filming funny sketches with my friends. I'm supposed to be home for dinner after swim practice. I'm supposed to still be flirting with boys who don't know I'm flirting with them! How was college not yesterday? Why can't I remember high school teachers' names as easily as I used to? Why do my parents look so old? When did I stop holding a grudge against friends who wronged me when I was twenty? What do I remember? Why can't I tell 2015, 2016, 2017, and 2018 apart? Does my adolescence kind of not matter anymore? Didn't I promise, like, five girls we'd be best friends forever? At nineteen, didn't I make a pact with Alex Feldman that if we were both single by the decrepit age of thirty that we would get married? Didn't he die or, like, move to Singapore? I don't know, I stopped checking Facebook (Meta, whatever) over a decade ago!

In my mind, there's still time.

In my mind, I still could wake up and become a different person. I can still move to Italy or France and work at a café and be young enough that it's considered attractive and quirky, versus being an older woman who has to work at a café to support herself. I could still get *really* in shape and be effortlessly glamorous when I travel. I could still learn a new language, and I could still be all the versions of myself I want to explore when my mind is racing and I'm trying to fall asleep.

In reality, who I am is mostly formed, or on its way to being mostly formed. I don't think anyone is ever fully formed. I'm not going to become someone new; I've always been me, I always will be. I'll just be a different version of me, especially now that I'm a mother. There is no French café in my future unless something goes horribly wrong with my current life.

In my mind, I'm still thinking about dating options and the kind of woman I could be in different couples.

In reality, I've been married for almost four years, and even in my daydreams I can't bring myself to cheat on my husband. He's never going to be an international DJ and I'm never going to follow him on his world tour.

In my mind, a Saturday night still holds mystery. I can still be a mystery. Who I meet and stay out with is still a mystery.

In reality? I'll do a few sets, and then Noah and I will drink orange wine together and watch *30 Rock* with the baby. I will be wearing a sweatshirt that has *a lot* of dog hair on it. And I'll relish every moment of that. Around eleven thirty, I'll ask if he's hungry, he'll say no, and I'll eat a handful of chocolate chips I keep in the back of the freezer for emergencies.

In my mind, driving across the desert is filled with small towns, heartbreak, the open road, and me draped over an outlaw who looks like a Ralph Lauren model.

In reality, we're in my husband's Ford Fusion Hybrid on the way to visit his brother, and we're listening to a podcast as I argue along . . . to a speaker.

In my mind, I'll be fashionable on this vacation, I'll have the perfect beach outfit and summer dining outfit, and I'll fit in effortlessly.

In reality? I don't have enough room to pack multiple shoe options and I think most resort wear is dorky and I think floral patterns are ugly and I don't care. I'm going to wear the same T-shirt three days in a row and I left my nice purse at home because I don't wanna ruin it on the trip. There's no reason to bring a Louis Vuitton to the beach. No leather on the beach!

In my mind, we might have two children; we may live abroad for a while before deciding on kids.

In reality, I'm thirty-nine and we just had a gorgeous baby girl and I think it would be terrible to move abroad and deprive all of our parents who are, thank God, still with us, the chance of seeing her as often as they do. Recently, I had a doctor's visit where I was told I needed to basically decide *today* if I want to have more than one kid in the future. In my mind, I had time.

In my mind, I don't care about mom jokes or mom life Instagram stories.

In reality, I know I'll become these things. I caught myself saying, "They have some *gorgeous fruit* at the buffet" yesterday to Noah. And then I said, "Hotel checkout was *easy peasy*." What. Is. Happening. To. Meeeeee.

In my mind, I'm chic. I decorate my house in design-forward, bold choices, terrazzo everything, lots of plants and vintage furniture. I have a massive picture of a naked woman smoking a cigarette because I'm very sexual!

In reality? I'll probably do a lot of gray hues and get a sturdy couch from Restoration Hardware. My router is out in the open.

In my mind? My skin is smooth, hydrated, and pretty wrinkle-free for being almost forty.

In reality? Those things are true, but it shocks me how tired I look even with a full night's sleep.

In my mind, I am totally alone. No one gets me 100 percent of the time; people are hard on me.

In reality, this is true, but it's selfish to pretend I'm doing life alone, because I am loved.

In my mind, I will one day become an APEX adult.

In reality, adulthood finds you. It finds you on the 405 as you rage-cry with mental exhaustion at a medical office phone tree designed to make sure you can never actually make an appointment.

In my mind, I can buy enough face serum to look like the women on Instagram do.

In reality? They don't even look that way, and I choose to keep buying into the lie. Because aging is inevitable, and fighting the signs is all we can do.

In my mind, I want to read every book, listen to every lecture, and educate myself about everything all the time.

In reality? Most people are boring, too many banal interviews and "ums" and irrelevant elaborations in most podcasts, and I skip ahead. Most people don't have new information and talk too damn slow. Also, doesn't it seem like it's all bad news these last few years? In my three minutes of free time I'd rather listen to Cascada's "Everytime We Touch" and hang out in my bathroom ironing patches onto my jacket. I need a break.

In my mind, I'm gonna make more time to talk to my mom, hear her thoughts and have her validate every thought I've ever had. To get her take on everything while I still have her.

In reality? I forget to do those things when she visits and we usually just argue about how my living room furniture is arranged and then we watch a movie together. It's perfect.

In my mind, I live among the redwoods, I'm barefoot often, and I do a lot of breathing. I'm zero-waste, I eat plant-based, I can name fifteen types of wild herbs, and I really take time to understand life.

In reality? I just threw a tuna can across the kitchen because it wouldn't open. And I don't go outside as often as I should because I can't control the temperature like I can inside my office. Also, the sun is bad for my aging skin!

In my mind, I'm always cutting idiots down with the perfect snipe.

In reality? Most people aren't worth it, so I end up not wasting my breath and just secretly wishing them dead and just talking a lot of shit later.

In my mind? People mean well and are pure at heart.

In reality? Most people are lying 100 percent of the time. Most people also mean well but are stupid.

In my mind is where a lot of fantasies and fear live.

In reality? It's only when I step outside of myself that I can truly experience life and appreciate how good things can be. All things aside, life can be wonderful if you set all things aside.

ALL THINGS ASIDE

What could be more apt in terms of really living the theme of *All Things Aside* than me being pregnant and having a baby *as* I was delivering this book? Was it all things aside: I'm having a baby and nothing else matters? Or was it: I'm having a baby and, all things aside associated with that, I still have other things to say?

I had Sierra and, overnight, my world shifted. In the weeks that followed her birth, it became impossible to think about anything other than my daughter. I couldn't really absorb anything I tried to read or watch or do.

In the weeks prior to her birth, I had tried to "relax" by reading historical fiction at night. Am I the only one who has trouble separating WWII historical fiction from the nonfictional fact that the very real Holocaust was simultaneously happening? I just find it very hard to focus on a narrative about, say, two lovers ripped apart by war when, just a few miles away, my people were being tortured and murdered. Like, if your story is set in Europe between 1933 and 1945 and it doesn't mention the Holocaust, I will just have that storyline running in my head the entire time, parallel to whatever you write. "On a gray day in mid-April, the haberdasher's daughter set out to—" Oh my God, I don't care because there is a death camp operating at full speed one town over! How am I supposed to care about her first kiss?

On the absolute other end of the spectrum, I also found it hard to read educational baby books. I wanted to be the kind of mom who read *everything,* mostly so that later in my child's life, when I stressed how much I loved her, I would be able to say, "I read every book there was!" But, instead, I've taken comfort in my new identity as the mom who read nothing, googled a few things, and everything was fine. Okay, not true, I read a bunch of parenting facts on Instagram. And I listened to my own mother's advice.

Of all the changes that happened to me while I was pregnant and after I gave birth, my brain turning into a "mom brain" was the hardest to accept. My ability to retain information had gotten so bad that when the pediatrician called about the baby, my husband said, "Why don't you put him on speaker so I can listen too, just in case?" I remember watching the *James Bond* movie *No Time to Die* and thinking, *How can anyone care about a poisonous plant terrorist plot when I just had a baby?!*

I watched the *Jackass Forever* movie and, while yes, of course I laughed every time one of them got hit in the dick, my second thought was, *His poor mother must feel so sad watching her son absolutely wreck his scrotum.*

In an instant I understood life differently. I understood what my mother had been talking about all these years. I understood why my friends with babies would send pics of their children, unprompted.

> This is an urge I fight and I encourage you to fight because, honestly? No one wants pictures of your child rapid-fired at them . . . aside from the grandparents. Other friends with children would do a bait-and-switch, like "Hey! Just checking in on you. How are you feeling? If you want some sunshine today, here's Brittley, let's pretend that's a normal name! She's on a slide! LOL." But I get it, we love our babies so much that we just want to share them. I felt this way about my dogs, so why wouldn't I feel this way about my child?

I understood self-sacrifice and I understood how easily mothers can be maligned in their pursuit of their child's happiness and well-being. Moreover, I understood how deeply personal and unique the journey into becoming a parent is while still being something all parents have in common.

And, above all of those colossal concepts, what I understood is that nothing anyone said needed to matter to me ever again because no one but her mattered.

> I had survived my pregnancy with self-imposed blinders on. I moved confidently toward my due date very in touch with who I was and what information I wanted to take in. Everyone has an opinion on how you handle your pregnancy. Every friend with a child has advice or warnings. I navigated all of that by mostly keeping to myself and purposefully seeking out the information I wanted. Never forget that women have been giving birth for thousands of years in horrific circumstances and

they got through it. You know what to do, your body knows what to do. And, barring anything life threatening, you are going to be pregnant and give birth and all you have to do is just give yourself over to it and do your best. There is an entire industry out there whose main goal is to convince you that you are helpless and clueless and your baby will be damaged if you don't drink their Power Mama Protein Packets and take their Genius Mama Bimbo Blip Blorp Pre-Natal Big Brain vitamins. You won't be able to handle your baby if you don't get the Morpheus Horpee 3000 Diaper Pail/Stroller/Pentium Processor/Swaddle Microwave and your kid will fall behind if you don't pry open their eyes and show them this Norwegian-made, neutral-toned picture book featuring only words printed in binary code! "The Cow says '1010.'"

One night while I was still pregnant and on another one of my eye-numbing Instagram info quest scroll sessions, I was force-fed this quote about motherhood that I *instantly* hated.

"They say if a woman's first child is a girl, she most likely needed maturity and if it's a boy, she most likely needed to know the real meaning of love."

WHO IS "THEY"?? The village elders? The comments section? People who have never had kids? Men passing pro-life legislation over shots of Everclear in a fucking duck blind?

The idea of a third party looking at me ("they" did specify "woman"—note they didn't say "girl," so it's fair that I assume they are making a blanket statement about all women) and deciding that what I was missing was maturity or the ability to understand love is so pejorative, so offensive, and speaks so specifically to the way we see women's intelligence.

Women are not little girls in need of lessons. We are not lost bumbling dolts in pigtails in need of direction from society, or a spanking, or a fucking *daddy*. What we need is equal pay. What we need is safety and respect. And what we need is to stop being told what we need.

I was very cautious in writing this book. I didn't want this to be a book about pregnancy or about being a mother. That's an entire ocean into which I've only dipped my toes; whether the waters are icy or warm and inviting remains to be seen. For the bulk of this book, I was careful to not overstep my boundaries when it came to parenting views, as a woman who hadn't actually had a child yet. But now that I'm writing this addendum, now that I've *had* my baby . . . I feel comfortable in presenting my opinion as fact when it comes to my specific experience. And what I want to say is less about my birthing experience and more about what I took away from it.

So, in the wake of having gone through labor, I will tell you: When it comes to giving birth, SO MUCH information belongs . . .

Down here, in the indentation. In the elaboration. In the aside. There are so many kinds of births and so many ways to become a parent. Having a baby is life-altering, there is no way you can take in all of the information, especially since so much of the information probably doesn't apply to you or is just an opinion. I looked up "best foods to eat while breastfeeding" and in three different articles I got "dairy products are bad," "dairy products are good," and "there are no foods that are particularly better." (And then I got an ad showing a cow being murdered.) So I guess don't eat paint and drink buckets of vodka and you should be okay? And you know what else? I breastfed but you bet I also supplemented with a fancy German imported formula *just in case she wasn't getting enough*. I think a lot of moms use formula and it just isn't talked about. The assumption is that the moment we give birth we have *gallons* of milk spewing forth, and breastfeeding is hard for *other* women. And formula is used only if you're okay with your kid being like, a little behind in life.

But I'll tell you right now: At first, when it was just colostrum, before the milk had come in? I was hand expressing tiny drops into a *spoon*, sucking them up with a plastic syringe and feeding them directly to her . . . like an adopted kitten. Spoons, syringes . . . it's like Noah and I were in *Trainspotting*.

I breastfed, I pumped, and sometimes if I needed a break or if she fed *forever* and was still hungry, we just warmed up some formula. The day they find the link between formula and serial killers, let me know (or you won't, because I'll already be murdered). Until then, all I know is I have a healthy, well-fed baby and I'm not interested in anyone's hot take, agreement, endorsement, etc. I simply want to share what I did and I don't need any feedback.

Personally, I like breastfeeding my daughter. I enjoy bonding with her, and it's the most natural thing in the world. Pumping is another story. Forget pain, it's just a plain WEIRD feeling.

You know what's hard to do? Focus on anything when your nipples are being *tweaked*. It's the most distracting thing in the world if you plan on fielding any other thoughts or emotions. Giving birth is a monumental task. And that's one thing. But OVERNIGHT you are supposed to shake off the messaging you've been subjected to your whole life; that breasts are not necessarily yours but rather that they exist as sexual objects to be enjoyed by others, admired by others, judged by others (and used *by you* to get free drinks). Now you have to instantly forge a new neural pathway where you endure nipple stimulation not as *foreplay*, but as a means of feeding an infant. I'd be pumping, watching something as banal as *The Great British Baking Show*, a warm bath of a TV program, something that's meant to invoke nothing but smiles and drooling, and I'd randomly become mentally irritated, which would trigger nervousness. Why? Because an unwanted physical/sexual experience will do that to a person! Particularly an intermittent one that you are forced to engage in several times a day that you aren't allowed to categorize as sexually triggering, and which no one talks about. See if a man could do it. Go up to a man, any man, or any person, and start twisting their nipples or like, full-on stroking their penis and then say, "I need you to tell me how much you love your mother and then recap your day." He would be very distracted and uncomfortable! That's how pumping feels. And yet, I was happy to do it. Because it was for my baby, who I love more than I love myself.

So what's the takeaway here at the end of the book? What's the revelation? I guess it's that, somehow, everything and yet nothing matters all at once. If things as huge as "space" and "time" can be seen as relative concepts, then surely everything else we fill our lives with like customer service, social rules, heartache, fashion, competition, taste, and the pursuit of success and happiness all have to be relative as well. All you have in this life that is totally and originally yours is your perspective on your true experiences. I've chosen to make my living and create my happiness by talking about my experiences to everyone about almost everything.

Because all things aside, our lives happen here, in the details.

ACKNOWLEDGMENTS

In these last few years, I've taken a hard look at success and my career and what those two things have in common.

I always acknowledge my fans, because without them I wouldn't have a career. But I'm taking this page and a half to acknowledge the intrepid team of people who have chosen to build their careers alongside mine. These are people who have bet on me and chosen to stay with me and support my creativity through the ups and downs on our way to the top. Because I'm not just an author, because I'm a comedian, all of the branches of my business intertwine, I wanted to thank some people in the context of this book.

My manager is who helps me and guides me to find the right people to work with.

> My manager, Kara Baker, has been with me since 2006. She was the first person to believe in me professionally and has helped shape a career I am very proud of. She's a big sister, a second set of eyes, and my protector.

My publicist is the reason new fans find me and old fans get to keep seeing me in new ways.

Greg Longstreet has been my publicist since 2010 and has helped create every campaign for every show, special, and book. He is intrepid in touting me to every press outlet and talent booker. He's a damn good publicist . . . and an okay friend too.

My literary agent is the reason this book got the attention from the right publisher.

Brandi Bowles was my literary agent on *Girl Logic* and stuck by me through several iterations of that book, other versions of other books that never saw the light of day, and this. I sent it to her out of the blue and she ran with it.

My touring agent is the reason I have bigger and bigger venues in which to perform for the fans who buy this book.

I met Joe Schwartz in 2014 *at* the taping of my second Netflix special. Since then, he has taken my career to new heights and, because of his guidance, it wasn't a rocket ship that fizzled out but a steady 757 that continues to climb.

My husband . . .

Noah had the idea to indent the asides. Even on a vacation you proofread my work. You emboldened me to write this book. I love you so much.

Through every win and every loss, every achievement that I don't think is good enough, and every failure that I make out to be a bigger deal than it actually is, this is the team that's right there cheering me on.

These people are the reason I have anything good in my career. Thanks, guys.